THE LANGUAGE LIBRARY

CHAMBER OF HORRORS

THE LANGUAGE LIBRARY

EDITED BY ERIC PARTRIDGE

★

GOOD ENGLISH: HOW TO WRITE IT

G. H. Vallins

CHAMBER OF HORRORS

A Glossary of British and American officialese, with an Introduction by Eric Partridge

'Vigilans'

THE ENGLISH LANGUAGE

With a chapter on the history of American English by Professor John W. Clark, of the University of Minnesota

Professor Ernest Weekley

‘VIGILANS’

CHAMBER OF HORRORS

A GLOSSARY OF OFFICIAL JARGON BOTH ENGLISH AND AMERICAN

WITH AN INTRODUCTION BY
ERIC PARTRIDGE

BRITISH BOOK CENTRE
NEW YORK

First published 1952

BRITISH BOOK CENTRE INC.
122 East 55th Street
New York 22, N.Y.

Printed in Great Britain by
TONBRIDGE PRINTERS LTD
Tonbridge Kent

TO

IVOR BROWN

GRACIOUS GUARDIAN OF ENGLISH

APPRECIATIVELY

'VIGILANS'

PREFACE

THE fungoid growth of jargon—defined by Mr Lane Norcott as 'the official language of the ruling classes'—shows few signs of dying out, despite the efforts of Sir Alan Herbert, Sir Ernest Gowers, Mr Eric Partridge and others. Admittedly there seems to have been a slight improvement among the higher-placed Civil Servants, but this is more than offset by the increase of bureaucracy. More Civil Servants and Local Government officers than ever are now using jargon.

It occurred to me, so long ago as 1945, that something should be done to check the spread of these weeds. Having a living to make, I was, at that time, unable to do much about it. But I have, at least, kept a note of the more noisome specimens and compared them with the horrible examples pilloried by the authorities mentioned above and in the ensuing list of Sources.

To Mr Eric Partridge I owe a special debt. He has encouraged and helped me in the search for jargon, brought to my notice the *Britannica Book of the Year*, the Funk and Wagnalls *New Standard Year Book* and Professor Evans's *The Use of English;* obtained—through the kindness of Professor Richmond Pugh Bond, Professor W. John Clark, Professor Mario A. Pei, Mr Horace Reynolds—many of the American examples; and written an Introduction. Indeed, I wonder why he did not elect to write the glossary also.

'VIGILANS'

May 29, 1952

SOURCES

Apart from various casually encountered Civil Service, Local Government, and 'Fighting Services' forms, and occasional references in the press of the past twenty years or so, the following are the principal sources of direct and indirect information.

Sir Arthur Quiller-Couch: *On the Art of Writing*, 1916: 'Interlude: On Jargon', a lecture delivered at Cambridge on May 1, 1913.

H. W. Fowler: *Modern English Usage*, 1926.

Sir Alan Herbert: *What a Word!*, 1935.

Funk and Wagnalls, *New Standard Encyclopedia Year Book* for 1942–51.

Britannica Book of the Year, 1944 to 1951: at 'Words and Senses, New'.

The Shorter Oxford Dictionary, edited by C. T. Onions, revised edition of 1944: 'Addenda'.

Webster's New International Dictionary, impression of 1945: 'New Words Section'.

George Orwell: 'Politics and the English Language', in *Horizon*, 1945; reprinted in *Shooting an Elephant*, 1950.

Professor J. Y. T. Greig: *Keep up the Fight for English*, 1946.

Eric Partridge: *Usage and Abusage: A Guide to Good English*, 1947.

Eric Partridge: *Words at War: Words at Peace*, 1948.

Sir Ernest Gowers: *Plain Words*, 1948.

James R. Masterson and Wendell Brooks Phillips: *Federal Prose*, 1948.

Eric Partridge: *English: A Course for Human Beings*, 1949.

Dr B. Ifor Evans: *The Use of English*, 1949.

Funk and Wagnalls: *New Standard Dictionary*, edition of 1949: 'Supplement'.

Peter Edson: 'Tops in Gobbledegook': in the *New York Sun*, January 7, 1950.

Eric Partridge and John W. Clark: *British and American English since 1900*, 1951.

SOURCES

Norman Riley: 'Dehydrated English': in *The Daily Telegraph*, July 14, 1951.

Anon., 'Optimum Wordage': in *Evening Standard*, August 17, 1951.

Sir Ernest Gowers, *A B C of Plain Words*, October 1, 1951.

Anon., 'Anti-Disincentivism': in *The Washington Post*, mid-October, 1951.

'Jackdaw': in *John o' London's Weekly*, October 23, 1951.

How to Prepare Your U.S. Income Tax Return for 1951, *on Form* 1040: U.S. Government Printing Office, 1951.

G. H. Vallins, *Good English: How to Write it*, revised and enlarged edition, 1952.

CONTENTS

INTRODUCTION

He was . . . full of jargon as a flecked pie (magpie)
Chaucer, *c. 1386*

With beast and bird the forest rings
Each in his jargon cries and sings
Longfellow, *1830*

All the incoherent jargon of the
schools (of medieval philosophy)
Swift, *1692*

1. THE MEANING OF JARGON

FROM the *jargoning* of birds to the jargon of Whitehall and Washington may seem a far cry. Yet, between the warbling and chattering of birds and the grave or the dulcet wooings, admonitions and instructions of officials, there exists a close kinship. Some of this 'talk' is unintelligible, some almost meaningless; much of it is loud-sounding, a little of it sonorous.

The English sense-development follows roughly this course:

(1) The warbling of birds, but also their chattering or twittering: 14th-15th centuries; hence or, more probably, direct from French—

(2) gibberish, nonsense: 14th–20th centuries; hence—

(3) barbarous or debased language: 17th–19th centuries;

(4) probably from a fusion of (2) and (3): any mode of speech that is either full of unfamiliar terms or peculiar to a set of persons (especially philosophers and other scholars) or to the terminology of a science or an art or to the technical vocabulary of a profession, a trade, a craft: late 17th–20th centuries; hence—

(5) 'language full of circumlocutions and long, high-sounding words' (*Webster*): late 19th–20th centuries;

(6) official jargon: 20th century. (The subject of this book.)

The reference to French needs to be amplified. Old French *jargon* or *jargoun* or *gargon*, warbling of birds, soon gained a subsidiary sense 'peculiar language' (for instance, of animals), whence, in the 15th century, the senses numbered (3) and (4) above. Akin to *gargouiller*, whence the English *gargle*, Old French *jargon* and its derivative verb *jargonner*, to warble, derive from a stem *garg-* (*jarg-* being a variant), which basically means 'throat'. Even *garg-* or *jarg-* can be carried one stage further: it forms an extended or modified form of European *gar-* or *ger-*, to cry out, itself a specialized derivative from an Indo-European *-guer*, to swallow, itself intimately related to or even making a pair with *guel-*, throat. In short, both *gargle* and *jargon*, nouns and verbs, denote '(to make) a noise in or with the throat' and connote '(to make) a queer noise in the throat'. The transition from the spoken to the written noise carries a further risk: that of the temptation to impress the eye no less than the ear.

The inter-relationship of senses (4), (5) and (6) is clearly so intimate as hardly to be analysable. Yet (6)—'official jargon'—now has certain definite and easily recognizable features of its own, including, by adoption, the two features that go to make of (5) a separate stage in the development of the various meanings of *jargon*. Official jargon also has a far from negligible vocabulary, if by 'vocabulary' one understands not only words but phrases, and not only phrases but turns of phrase. With that very odd vocabulary 'Vigilans' has dealt in the ensuing pages.

2. THE NAMES FOR JARGON

'Official jargon' has other names, the commonest being simply 'jargon': *hereinafter*, 'jargon' is to be understood in that sense. When, in 1913, Sir Arthur Quiller-Couch delivered, at Cambridge, his famous lecture 'On Jargon', he meant both (5) and (6). 'Q' defined the term as 'that infirmity of speech—that flux, that determination of words to the mouth, or to the pen—which, though it be familiar to you in parliamentary debates, in newspapers, and as the staple language of Blue Books, Committees, Official Reports, I take leave to introduce to you as prose which is not prose and under its real name of Jargon'. He continues: 'You must not confuse this jargon with what is called Journalese. The two overlap, indeed, and have a knack of assimilating each other's vices.' Less, yet still notable, is the deleterious interaction of jargon and commercialese or, as Sir Alan Herbert called it, officese.

Official jargon and its elliptical synonym, *jargon*, are the names preferred by scholars. Yet there are others. In several books I have tried to popularize my own term for it: *officialese*. That term, I notice, has now drawn almost level with *jargon* and, among others than scholars, has beaten *official jargon* into third place.

Then there is Mr Ivor Brown's *barnacular*, a blend of *barnacle*, typifying the Civil Servant, who tends to stick like that unlovely crustacean to the bottom of the Ship of State, and of *vernacular*. But the term is much too witty for it to have won a general acceptance.

Slightly more popular is *Whitehallese*; it ranks next to *jargon*, *officialese*, *official jargon*. The name has wit, for it connotes 'the journal*ese* of *Whitehall*'—that is, of the Ministries and Departments so conveniently brought, at least theoretically, into that sub-district of Westminster.

All these names are British. In the United States of America, both *jargon* and *official jargon* are occasionally used; so too, though perhaps less, are *officialese* and *Whitehallese*. But the two entirely American names[1] for official jargon are *Federal prose* and *gobbledygook* (occasionally spelt *gobbledegook*). The former obviously refers to the prose favoured by the officials of the Federal Government, which works from Washington. It has been defined as 'that form of nonmetrical composition, apparently English, which can be invariably interpreted as meaning

[1] Of Paul R. Porter's edict against jargon—see the reference to him at *dichotomy*—the author of 'Anti-Disincentivism', a delightful editorial in *The Washington Post*, October 15 (?), 1951, commiserates with him thus: 'He is trying to have the English language adopted as the official idiom of the Federal Government, and to do away with the two prevailing dialects, which are known to philologists as Demotic Gobbledygook and Hieratic Federalese.' I wish I could quote this 'leader' in its entirety, for it shows a perfect mastery of urbane and scholarly irony.

and/or not meaning more and/or less than, rather than what, it seems to mean'.[1]

Gobbledygook, however, is more interesting. In *The New York Times* of April 12, 1946, Arthur Krock spoke of 'the mumbling language of bureaucracy, a kind of Washington Choctaw against which Maury Maverick some years ago erupted violently and named "gobbledygook" '. The *Britannica Book of the Year* 1945 (published in 1946) attributes the word to the Hon. Maury Maverick and states that the year of the eruption was 1944. The inclusion in the 'New Words and Senses' section of that year-book constitutes one of the earlier semi-official recognitions of the word as part of Standard American English, but it had almost immediately won that status: when a term is so devastatingly apposite as *gobbledygook*, it walks unquestioned into the vocabulary, as *quisling* had done four years earlier in Britain.

The allusion is to the gobbling noise made by a turkey cock; probably the word was an unconscious yet none the less inspired adaptation of '*gobble* of *the* turkey *cock*', *the* becoming *de* in imitation of stage foreigners' pronunciation and *cock* becoming *gock* by assimilation to the *g* of *gobble* and *gock* becoming *gook* perhaps under the influence of *goon*. A turkey cock is pompous and its gobble resembles an unintelligibly guttural speech. The Hon. Maury Maverick, of Texas, a descendant of that other well-known Texan who has bestowed a word upon the language, the cattle-owner Samuel A. Maverick, himself, in *The New York Times* of May 21, 1944, explained the term thus: 'People ask me where I got gobbledygook. I do not know. It must have come in a vision. Perhaps I was thinking of the old bearded turkey gobbler back in Texas, who was always gobbledy-gobbling and strutting with ludicrous pomposity. At the end of this gobble there was a sort of gook.'

Common to both British and American jargon is the specialized form that, since at least as early as April 1947, has been called *economese*. Economese has perpetrated some of the worst

[1] James R. Masterson & Wendell Brooks Phillips, *Federal Prose. How to Write in and/or for Washington*, an ironically witty pamphlet, published in 1948 by The University of North Carolina Press.

of all the many crimes committed by the jargoneers. 'Vigilans' has dealt with some of them; I need only mention such examples as *adjustments to economic conditions*, usually preceded by *necessary*; *bottleneck*; the American *carryback* and *rollback*; *disincentive*; *feather-bedding*. To mention any more would be to spoil the fun.

3. THE NATURE OF JARGON

It is, however, fatally easy to generalize without bringing forward such evidence as will justify the generalizations. But jargon could not be adequately exemplified without reducing the reader to a fatal degree of boredom.

Sir Alan Herbert in *What a Word!* (1935), and Sir Ernest Gowers in *Plain Words* (1948), have quoted some delectable—that is, horrifying—examples. These examples, like those quoted by the late George Orwell in a famous article ('Politics and the English Language'), and by Dr B. Ifor Evans in *The Use of English* (1949), are perhaps too well known to bear being reprinted. But in a spirited pamphlet, too little known outside South Africa, *Keep up the Fight for English* (1946), Professor J. Y. T. Greig has, from 'an interim report issued by a South African Commission', quoted a passage of which he wryly says, 'All my attempts to translate this into English have failed'. Here it is:

'Legal opinion has been taken in regard to whether, in the event of such amendments being made, there would be any possibility of a successful claim being lodged against superannuation benefits by any party other than the Administration in respect of any amount that might be outstanding at the time of a servant's retirement or death, or of his leaving the service for any reason, in respect of property purchased from monies obtained from some source other than the Administration, or on any other account. The opinion is to the effect that no difficulty should be experienced in drafting the proposed amendments to cover the phases mentioned and in such a way as to limit the right to reimbursement from benefits accruing under the Act, to the Administration only, and solely for the purpose contemplated.'

The trouble is that the writer has failed to develop his thought clearly.

Here is an easier piece of jargon:

'I ventured to draw your attention last year to the beneficial effect upon the economic condition of South Africa which might be anticipated from any sustained improvement in world trade and in the prices of the staple products emanating from the Union.'

Upon this, Professor Greig comments: 'Not very pretty, is it?' He renders it into English:

'I ventured to suggest to you last year that South Africa would improve economically if world trade increased and the prices of staple South African products rose.'

For the first seven words of the English version I should myself substitute 'Last year I suggested'. Such modesty rings false.

But the United States of America can show examples no less formidable. In the *New York Sun* of January 7, 1950, Peter Edson quoted the first two sentences of a pamphlet that had just come into his hands, a Federal publication with the delusively promising title, *Business and Government*, a report drawn up by 'the President's Council of Economic Advisers'. These two sentences run—if 'run' be the right word—thus:

'The balance emphasis which the Employment Act places upon the merits and responsibilities of free enterprise and free government is typically American and yet of universal import at this midpoint in the 20th century. In the last century the philosophic base was laid for extremist doctrines that these two freedoms were irreconcilable, and that one or the other give way under the impact of industrial concentration, disparate wealth and popular communication.'

No wonder Mr Edson heads his article: 'Tops in Gobbledegook Is Just About Reached'. Yet I prefer an earlier example, quoted by Frank Aston in the *New York World Telegram* of April 6, 1946:

'Looking toward an ultimate co-ordination and implementation of heretofore diversified innerdepartmental practices regarding the briefing of smaller consumers relative to their allotment status, it has been determined that there will be conducted Thursday next at eight o'clock a panel discussion in which will be . . .'

Mr Aston, writing from Washington, had begun his article with some entertaining information:

'The government promises again to drive for a simpler language. The Civil Service Commission is instructing federal writers in clarity and brevity. . . .

'Civil Service is shooting at gobbledygook. That term is applied to lingo that has grown up in departments, bureaus and agencies. Among its peculiarities are long sentences of awkward construction and uncommon words.'

From the same article we learn that 'Civil Service has issued a pamphlet, "How Does Your Writing Read?" It is available to all government writers.'

'Some bureaucrats have taken the hint and organized classes. They criticize each other's writing and listen to experts lecture on sensible English.'

But that was so long ago as April 1946. Mr Edson's letter of January 1950, and Sir Ernest Gowers's book,[1] first published in April 1948, have shown—if we needed to be shown—that, despite the efforts of able and zealous reformers, British and American jargon still flourishes. Perhaps slightly fewer Civil Servants are using it; certainly those still using it wallow in an officialese almost as lush as ever it was.

Except that it is more cautious and circumlocutory than the jargons of artists and authors, scientists and psychiatrists, officialese inevitably shows the defects noticeable in those other jargons. After all, it is precisely these defects which, in the aggregate, make jargon what it is. Officialese has not shown any marked desire to be different from its fellows.

The predominant characteristics of jargon in general and of official jargon, or officialese, in particular, are perhaps those:

(1) Circumlocution, as in 'He will cause inquiries to be instituted'—or 'investigations to be initiated'—'with a view to ascertaining the views of the general public upon the subject of national dietary standards,' which means

[1] All unspecified references to Sir Ernest Gowers concern *Plain Words*, not *ABC of Plain Words*.

'He will find out what people think about the national diet'. The 'Official' sentence exemplifies also a trait even more prevalent than circumlocution: and that is—

(2) the use of long words for short, abstract for concrete, unfamiliar for familiar, and Latin (occasionally Greek) for English, as *acquire* for *get*, *purchase* for *buy*, *communicate (with)* for *say* or *write* or *tell*, *desiderata* for *needs*.

(3) Phrases for single words, as *leave out of consideration* for *omit* or *forget*, *the majority of* (e.g., electors) for *most* (electors), *on the subject of* for *on* or *about*.

(4) Padding, as in *I venture to say* for *I say*, *it is incumbent upon those of us who are present to bear in mind the following considerations* for *we must remember*, and *it will be noted that something-or-other . . .* for *something-or-other*.

(5) Caution and euphemism. (Usually the euphemism expresses the caution, whether politic or truly considerate.) *It has been suggested that you might care to examine the enclosed documents* = *it is advisable for you to examine . . .* = *please examine*. Sir Ernest Gowers, in quoting from *The Times* part of a sentence from a Government department's letter to its advisory council, has supplied an example so delicious that it can hardly be omitted here:

'In transmitting this matter to the Council the Minister feels that it may be of assistance to them to learn that, as at present advised, he is inclined to the view that, in existing circumstances, there is, prima facie, a case for . . .'

Sir Ernest does not give us an equivalent in English. That equivalent is:

'The Minister wishes the Council to know that he thinks there is a case for . . .'

(6) Vagueness and woolliness, as in *the guarantee of a cessation of bulk-buying might be construed as militating against the interests of totalitarianism* = *by guaranteeing an open market we might expose ourselves to a charge of being individualists* = *if we guarantee an open market we shall perhaps be thought anti-social*; *the position with regard to food-consumption exhibits a maximum of non-availability* = *food is in short supply* = *food*

is scarce. The abstract for the concrete, the circumlocutory for the direct, make inevitably for vagueness and woolliness; clearly, then (6) is very closely linked to (1).

(7) Less important because much less frequent is the esoteric. Here we have abracadabra of a very special kind: the deliberate employment of technicalities, especially technicalities with a sense not easily deducible from the everyday meaning of the word. We see this strange principle at work not only in patently erudite terms, such as *virement*, *unilateral*, *terminus ad quem*, *technological*, *sterilize*, but also in apparently simple words, such as *rollback*, *down-turn*, *cutback*.

Behind these, the chief features of jargon, there lie the need for a certain degree of impersonality, the laudable desire to remain dispassionate, the less laudable but more natural desire to impress others, a regard for dignity, and, in a few officials, an attempt at euphony. The danger is that there may also be pomposity and 'more sound than sense' and a too persistent dread of committing oneself.

ERIC PARTRIDGE

CHAMBER OF HORRORS

A

ab initio. From the beginning; hence, at the beginning. Merely the first of the many unnecessary Latinisms included in this glossary. There are others—less known and, if that be possible, even more unnecessary.

ablution facilities. 'Do not say . . . *ablution facilities* for *wash basins*,' as Sir Ernest Gowers enjoins his fellow Civil Servants. Whereas the late H. W. Fowler had stigmatized the word *ablutions* as an example of Pedantic Humour, Eric Partridge calls *perform one's ablutions* 'a sorry jest'.

above, adjective. Borrowed from commercialese and elliptical for 'above-mentioned', as in 'The above information should be sufficient for your requirements'.

abstract, noun. A *summary* or *précis* of a letter, a report, a document, or of a self-contained passage; the *abridgement* of a pamphlet, a White Paper or a Blue Book. Equally official is 'to *abstract*', to *summarize*, or to *précis*, or to *abridge*. The word can be justified on etymological grounds—but only on etymological grounds.

accede to (a request). To grant (it).

accommodation unit. See **feeding-point.**

account. See **leave out of**—and **take into—account.**

acquaint. As a synonym for 'to tell', *acquaint* affords us a characteristic example of official dignity. 'You should acquaint us with the facts' seems feeble beside 'You should tell us the facts'. Compare **communicate, inform, state.**

acquire is a dignified officialism for either 'to get' or 'to gain' or even 'to buy'. In Eric Partridge's *Usage and Abusage* we hear of a Civil Servant wishing to be supplied, for official purposes, with a certain book and being told that he could 'acquire the work in question by purchase through the ordinary trade channels'—to buy it from a bookseller.

acreage in its strict sense 'area measured in acres' is clearly permissible. What one does object to is its use as a synonym for 'area' without '(number of) acres' understood. Norman Riley has pilloried it in the phrase 'the scheduled grazing acreage'.

action committee; activist. Belonging to communist political jargon, these words mean (*activist*) a member of an *action committee*, appointed to rid communist organizations of all non-communist persons, the purpose being to strengthen a potential communistic programme or revolution.

activate; activation. *Activate* and its noun *activation* are legitimate as terms in chemistry but jargonic in the senses 'to establish', and especially 'to establish and set going', e.g., an army division or an air squadron. To these Service usages, one objects but little; one does, however, object to the senses 'to get busy on' and 'to work hard at', as in 'to activate a reconversion program' (see the 1944 *Britannica Book of the Year*). So far, rarely used in Britain.

active consideration, under. '*The question is under active consideration* does not, or should not, mean anything more than that it is *under consideration*,' Sir Ernest Gowers. Many would prefer 'The question is *being considered*'.

activist. See *action committee.*

adequate standard of living. Enough money, especially of earnings. In an American governmental pamphlet, *Business and Government*, issued late in 1949, we find this gem: 'In an economy foredoomed to inability to provide an adequate standard of living for all industrious families there might be some reason for according the reshaping of output priority over efforts to increase output.'

ad hoc. For this specific purpose; pertinent to—or, for the sake of—this case, this question, this matter, alone; purposely. The Latin phrase means literally 'to, or for, this'. The Latin is shorter than the English could possibly be: that, however, does not justify its retention.

adjunct (American). A tool; an implement. Compare **agency.**

adjust (one's) **dress.** To button one's fly. 'You are requested to adjust your dress before leaving.' Only men see this notice, so why not use plain English? Moreover, the words *button one's fly* are offensive only to the prurient.

adjustments to economic conditions, the necessary; adjustments to new situations. The former, which occurred in some British periodical in 1951 (and often in 1950 and 1949, no doubt), means little more than *adaptability* or perhaps *good sense.* The latter appeared in the American pamphlet *Business and Government,* cited at **adequate standard** . . . and elsewhere, and connotes much the same thing; see the quotation at **interstitially.**

administrative democracy (American). Bureaucracy.

admit with regret. Sir Ernest Gowers has remarked upon this formula. It seldom means more than *to regret* or, usually, to *admit.* In other words, *admit with regret* too often is either excessive or insincere.

adumbrate is recorded in the list of 'Literarisms' in Eric Partridge's *Usage and Abusage* (New York, 1942; London, 1947). Since those days, however, the term has crept into official jargon in the senses 'to outline; to sketch' and, occasionally, 'to indicate only very partially, to announce vaguely'.

ad valorem. Literally, at its value—or, according to the value. Applied to a duty or other charge estimated according to a certain invoice; or to a tax assessment. *At*—or *on*—or *by*—or *according* to—*its*, or *the*, *value* would be English, therefore preferable to Latin; and is at least as clear.

advert. 'Do not say *advert* for *refer*,' enjoins Sir Ernest Gowers in *Plain Words*. Perhaps more precisely: 'Do not say *advert to* for *refer to*'—as in 'I shall advert to the matter when a more suitable occasion arises'.

advise. To tell; to mention; to announce. 'As advised in our letter . . .' This piece of commercialese has invaded the bureaucratic vocabulary, not to its advantage.

affirmative, in the. See **negative.**

affirmative facilitation. See **facilitate.**

agency (American). Loosely for 'tool' or 'implement'.

agenda. Business—or business to be discussed: points of discussion; or, as Sir Alan Herbert suggests, 'things to be done'. Like *advise*, this is primarily commercialese; like *advise*, it has invaded the jargon of Whitehall.

agreement, be in. To agree. 'For once, the members of the Housing Committee were in agreement'; 'The Ministry of —— is in agreement with the Ministry of ——'. This wordy phrasal verb occurs also in commercialese and was perhaps adopted from it.

allocation; allocator, allocatee. In official jargon, *allocation* bears a specific sense: 'government apportionment and distribution of available materials among producers of goods' (*Webster's*). Would it be over-fastidious to suggest that this definition might perhaps read: 'government apportionment [or, sharing-out] of materials among manufacturers'? An *allocatee* is a recipient of such materials; *allocator*, the person authorizing the apportionment.

alternative. The adjective *alternative*—not to be confused with *alternate*—is often used by Civil Servants to the detriment of such simple words as *other*, *different*, *new*, *fresh*, as Sir Ernest

Gowers has said; Sir Ernest has noticed that pair of Siamese twins, *alternative accommodation.*

Of the noun *alternative,* in its relationship to *choice,* the author of *Usage and Abusage* has written, 'The latter can be applied to any number, whereas *alternative* may be applied to only two courses of action—two possible decisions. "The alternatives are death with honour and exile with dishonour"; "He had the choice between fighting, running away, and capture"; "The alternative is to . . ."; "If you don't do that, you don't necessarily have to do this, for there are several choices". Strictly, therefore, "the *only* alternative" is tautological.'

ambulant. 'In my lifetime I have seen the *mad-doctor* pass through the chrysalis of *alienist* into the butterfly of *psychiatrist.* This is perhaps excusable, but why have *walking cases* suddenly become *ambulants?*' as Sir Ernest Gowers has so pertinently and suavely asked. The reason, one fears, is that *walking cases* was far too clear and simple.

ameliorate; amelioration. 'To ameliorate—or, amelioration of—the conditions of the inmates has always been the aim, the avowed aim, of the Board of Guardians.' To better, or to improve, the conditions—or improvement of the conditions—has always been the aim of . . . (Superior, however, is: The—Board of Guardians has always aimed to better, or improve, the . . .).

amount. Quantity; number. As officialese, more prevalent in North America than in Britain.

ancillary. Secondary; subsidiary. 'Accommodation . . . needed for the purposes ancillary to education—i.e. medical inspection and treatment, and school meals': the Minister of Education, 20 May 1951.

and/or. In *ABC of Plain Words,* Sir Ernest Gowers writes pungently about 'this ugly and unnecessary symbol'. If its use in lists and specifications can be defended, although even there it tends to save space at the expense of clarity, *and/or* should never appear either in letters or in documents intended for the general public. It can be avoided in at least six ways, thus:

(1) Officers *and/or* men should apply to Headquarters = Officers *and* men—or, *Both* officers *and* men—should apply to Headquarters;

(2) In a foreign ship *and/or* country, care must be taken to obey the laws = *Whether* in a foreign ship *or* in a foreign country, you should obey the laws; or—

(3) In a foreign ship, *as* in a foreign country, you . . .; or—

(4) In a foreign ship *or* country, you . . .;

(5) Soldiers *and/or* airmen will travel by rail = Soldiers *or* airmen *or both* will travel by rail.

(6) Applications will be considered from men *and/or* women = Applications will be considered from *either* men *or* women.

After all, *and/or* is a mere typographical device; it belongs to symbolography—not to style, nor yet to composition.

angle, from every. See **from every angle.**

angle of, from the. See **from the standpoint . . . of.**

animal protein factor. 'A vitamin complex in which vitamin B12 is a dominant factor' (I. Willis Russell in the *Britannica Book of the Year* 1950). In itself, this compound term belongs to scientific jargon, but unfortunately it is of the sort that Government dieticians are so ready to adopt and popularize.

anterior to. Before. By officialdom, it is held to be even more dignified than **prior to.**

anticipate, to forestall (etc.), should not be used as a synonym for 'to *expect*'. This piece of loose English, although strangely popular in the Civil Service, is not peculiar to officialese. See especially 'Fowler' and 'Partridge' on usage.

apartheid. A political policy (especially that of Dr Malan in South Africa) of racial segregation. Why not *segregation?* (*Apartheid* is Afrikaans for 'apartness'—'separation'.)

appear. To seem.

application of social principles, by the. The simple meaning soon emerges if you read, slowly and with due solemnity, this passage from an American governmental pamphlet, *Business and Government*, pilloried by Peter Edson in an article appearing on January 7, 1950: 'Contending individuals or groups in a free society could never arrive at viable agreements as to what share of national income each should get by the unalloyed application of social principles.' As an American might say, 'Can you *tie* that?'

applications are invited for the post(s), or **position**(s) **of,** e.g., **surveyor**(s). Surveyor(s) wanted. Perhaps it is unfair to cite, as official jargon, this particular example of verbosity; the fault occurs as frequently in the annals of Big Business as in those of Local Government, and much more frequently in both than in those of the Civil Service proper.

apportioned on the basis of percentage figures. Equitably apportioned; fairly distributed or awarded; assessed proportionately.

appreciable, appreciably. Both the adjective and the adverb occur rather often in officialese. Sometimes they are not needed at all; usually, however, a more precise word is demanded. In both respects, they closely resemble **considerable** (*considerably*) and **substantial** (*substantially*); moreover, these three words are often interchanged as if they were synonymous.

appreciate. This verb is rather too often used passively (*it will be appreciated that . . .*) instead of actively (*you will appreciate*) and far too often used as mere padding. Sir Ernest Gowers warns his juniors thus: '*It is appreciated that* (anticipating an objection that is to be met) and *it will be appreciated that* (introducing a reason for a decision that is to be given) are very prevalent. They can almost always be omitted altogether without harm to the sense, and with benefit to the style.'

There is another objection: *appreciate* is much vaguer than *understand* on the one hand and *see* or *realize* on the other.

apprehended that, it is. When Whitehall uses this circumlocution, it does so, not in the philosophical or the psychological senses nor in the common-or-garden sense 'it is feared', but for 'it is supposed', itself impersonal and remote for 'I suppose' or, for instance, 'the Minister supposes'.

appropriate, adjective. Officials prefer it to *right* or *fitting* or *suitable* because it is long and Latin and, in several of its connotations, legal; they are on surer ground when they prefer it to *special* ('In its appropriate and strictest sense').

Sometimes the word is used inaccurately, as in 'On the appropriate occasions, ceremonial robes will be worn'=On certain formal occasions, ceremonial robes . . .

appropriate, verb. To *appropriate* is not always synonymous with *take,* as every self-respecting writer knows: yet (despite their obvious share of self-respect) too many Civil Servants write as if it were.

Properly, *appropriate* is 'to take to oneself or for oneself alone'. In current usage, however, it predominantly means 'to set aside, formally, a sum of money for a specific purpose'.

approximate, approximately. *Approximately* is a long word for *roughly* or *about; approximate,* proportionately as long for *rough,* as in 'an approximate estimate' (a rough estimate) and 'in approximately three months' (in about three months).

So too for the verb: 'The total approximates to 1,000,000' =The total is roughly (or, about) 1,000,000' or '. . . comes to about . . .'

a priori, adverb and, derivatively, adjective. Deductive(ly); presumptive(ly) or presumable, presumably; without (detailed) examination—or without (sufficient) consideration. The Latin phrase is shorter than its English equivalents: but it is not English and it is often less clear than those equivalents.

as and from. See **as from.**

as and when. Either *as* or *when* does the work. 'As and when the plan becomes a fact, official recognition will follow' = When the plan, etc. Compare **if and when.**

as at present advised. So far as I, we, know or as he knows. '*As at present advised* should be used only where an opinion has been formed on expert (i.e. legal) advice,' Sir Ernest Gowers.

ascertain. To find out. See also **with a view to.**

as far as—is concerned. Sheer padding, as in 'As far as coffee is concerned, it does not suit everybody'=Coffee disagrees with some.

as from. From; since—or after. 'As from 1 July the salary has been £750 *per annum*' =Since July 1, the salary has been £750 a year. 'As from January 1, 2000, the appointment will no longer exist' = The appointment will end on January 1, 2000. Sir Ernest Gowers (*ABC*) disgustedly mentions the variant *as and from*, which is sheerest lunacy.

assist. To *help* or to *aid*. *Assist* probably appeals to officials because, unlike *help*, it is of Latin origin; because it has six letters to *aid*'s three; and because, despite its mildly suggestive sibilance, it sounds dignified.

assumption, a not unjustifiable. See **in my opinion . . .**

as to; especially, **as to whether.** (The unspeakable *in regard to whether* is happily less frequent.)

In 1916 'Q' described *according as to whether* as one of the 'dodges of Jargon, circumlocutions for evading this or that simple statement'.

In 1925 H. W. Fowler had some very good things to say

about it—including its correct use (*As to Smith, it is impossible to guess what line he will take*), which is still wordy; better: *It is impossible to tell what line Smith will take*, or *Smith? It is . . . he will take.*

In 1936 A. P. H. sparkled.

In 1942 (and 1947) Eric Partridge, indicting himself, showed that *as to* can often be written *of.*

In 1948 the author of *Plain Words* spoke very plainly.

Advice to those about to marry *as to:* Don't!

attached hereto. Tautological for *attached.*

at the due date. When due; when it was (is, will be) due.

attired. Clothed. The word attracts the genteel by its elegancy and the official by its dignity (perhaps a little shop-worn) and sonority; it is beginning to become slightly archaic and has already become more than slightly pompous.

B

background. One's past or qualifications or abilities. 'A man with such a background'—or 'such an educational background' (both tautological and ambiguous)—'would be better employed as an Education Officer.' Sir Ernest Gowers (*ABC*) is eloquent on *background.*

backlog. Arrears, whether of orders or applications or paper work. This extraordinarily inept application of a good domestic word perhaps came to England from the American armed forces; more probably, however, Whitehall took it from Washington which took it from (American) commercialese which has, for years, used it in the sense 'unfulfilled orders'.

[**barnacular.** See Introduction.]

basic. See **foundation,** adjective.

[**basic milk producer** has been ironically proposed by Norman Riley as preferable to *cow.* Please don't go putting ideas into their heads, Mr Riley! Some of these humourless creatures might take you seriously.]

basis. 'We do not work whole-time, but "on a whole-time basis", Sir Alan Herbert in 1935; for an example valid for 1948 (and still), see, at **proposition,** the sentence quoted by Sir Ernest Gowers. Here, *basis* has no justification at all: usually it is made, incorrectly, to bear the sense 'plan' or 'method'; and it leads to an irritating verbosity. In 1935 Sir Alan Herbert cited several damning examples. He labelled one of them *First Prize—Diploma*: 'The Labour Party must be built up on a rock-bottom basis.'

beddage. Beds collectively, especially in a hospital. 'If a hospital committee goes on writing and talking about "beddage", how long will it be before the little job of putting on a shirt button is called "sewage"?': Norman Riley in *The Daily Telegraph*, July 14, 1951. The *Evening Standard*, some five weeks later, showed that the atrocity committed by this hospital was even worse than the most pessimistic among us had feared: 'Accommodation at Welshpool Hospital did not represent "optimum beddage".' If you can bear to do so, please turn to **optimum.**

beg to acknowledge—to inform. Simply, to acknowledge or to inform (i.e. tell or say). Originally, I think, 'pure' commercialese, *beg to* was, long ago, adopted by Civil Servants, who have been using it rather less since Sir Ernest Gowers spoke firmly to them about it.

beverage. 'Hot and cold beverages may be purchased in the firm's canteen': that is, drinks. Fowler called *beverage* a 'stylish' word, *drink* a 'working' word. Beverage has insinuated its partly genteel, partly snobbish way into official jargon.

bifurcation. 'There was a time when, instead of "bifurcation", we should have used some simple, native cliché like "at the parting of the ways". But even clichés these days must be pretentious to be acceptable,' Norman Riley in *The Daily Telegraph*, July 14, 1951. Why not *fork?* And, also as a verb, *fork* is preferable to the erudite *bifurcate.*

bilateral or **bi-lateral.** Applied especially to an agreement or a contract, a treaty or a pact. Literally 'two-sided', the word is often used unnecessarily: there have to be at least two parties—and, oddly enough, two is the usual number. Sometimes, however, there are three or more parties (cf. **multilateral**). For an absurdity even worse than *bilateral,* see *unilateral.*

blanket, adjective and verb. All-inclusive; to cover all kinds and contingencies—to cover, or apply to, uniformly, no matter how diverse the objects or activities concerned. 'The President has introduced legislation that blankets all subversive acts, especially espionage and sabotage.' Gobbledygook; not unknown in Britain.

blue-print (English), **blueprint** (American), noun and verb. A plan, a scheme, a policy; to plan. The noun—much the commoner—has been described as 'one of those vogue words which have been spawned by officialdom and journalism acting in unholy conjunction. Strictly, a diagrammatic plan (white lines, etc., on blue paper), a technical scheme, it was already in 1941 in America . . . and by 1942 in Britain the fashionable word for political, social, military plans, with a connotation of doctrinaire infallibility. "A blueprint for invasion"—"a blueprint for victory"—and (what a laugh!) "blue-print for the New Britain" ' (Eric Partridge, *Usage and Abusage*, p. 350). A year later, Sir Ernest Gowers included it in a list of words 'overworked in official documents', thus: 'Blue-print: Plan'.

bona fide; bona fides. In good faith; good faith—hence, credentials, trustworthiness. There seems to be no good reason for preserving these Latin phrases.

bottleneck. Any such department or factory as causes difficulties, especially a delay either in the delivery or in the manufacture of goods. Like *target*, this shows the danger and exemplifies the harm in putting an admirably objective metaphor to non-objective uses, as in 'an economic system of interdependent bottlenecks' (to modify a ludicrous example quoted by Mr Henry Strauss).

brackets. *Bracket* for an income-tax *group* arose or, at the least, became general Civil Service jargon soon after the Second World War. It began its insidious career harmlessly enough as an Inland Revenue term, but before the end of 1948 it had been adopted by journalists, and others, who should have known better. The word derives from the vinculum (}) or bracket which, among Inland Revenue officials, serves to bring several trades or professions under one head.

breakdown has, since 1945 or so, been popular officialese for 'classification' or 'division' (or 'subdivision') or, specifically, 'division of a manufacturing process or job into distinct stages', or, more generally, 'analysis'. See especially Sir Ernest Gowers, *ABC of Plain Words* and *Webster's* (New Words).

breeder reactor. See **reactor.**

brief, verb; **briefing,** noun. To instruct, in detail, those about to engage in a military or, especially, an air operation. Hence, in official jargon, to do the same for one about to set off to a diplomatic or important trade conference or parley. In the *New York World Telegram* of April 6, 1946, Frank Aston alludes to the Civil Service Commission's implied objection to the occurrences of *briefing* in a governmental paper.

bring to a satisfactory conclusion. 'The whole complicated affair will, it is permissible to hope, be ultimately brought to a satisfactory conclusion'=Perhaps this complicated affair will at last (or, finally) be settled. George Orwell includes it in his list of 'resounding commonplaces' employed to save the ends of sentences from anticlimax. Compare **deserving of serious consideration.**

built-in inflation. This piece of gobbledygook has been severely criticized, even in its country of origin: see the quotation at **ratiocination.**

by reason of. Because of; through; by. 'Incapacitated by reason of infirmity'=disabled by infirmity.

Sir Ernest Gowers has shown that for *incapacitated* it is often better, especially in official forms addressed to ill-educated persons, to substitute (*rendered*) *unable to work.*

C

canalize. To set (something) along a certain path—to lead in the direction desired—in order to regulate or even to control (it). *The Shorter Oxford Dictionary*, 1944, dates its appearance at 1922. In American jargon, the word is *channelize*.

Hence, *canalization* (e.g., of resources) and *channelization.*

cannibalize; hence **cannibalization.** *Webster's* claims *cannibalize* for America, where, it is said, the term began as military slang for 'to collect and adapt as replacements (parts) from disabled machines or salvage of wrecks, for assembling a usable vehicle, aircraft, or the like; hence to dismantle for the sake of parts to be used for replacement'. *Cannibalize*, however, was so used in the R.A.F. at least as early as 1942, not as slang but as a technicality—a perhaps humorous development from the literal sense, 'to practise cannibalism'.

capable of [verbal noun]; **capable of locomotion.** Able to (e.g. do); able to walk. The latter has been, by Sir Ernest Gowers, included in a list of pomposities and circumlocutions to be avoided by self-respecting Civil Servants. 'He should by now be capable of making his own decisions'=He should be able to decide for himself. (Even *now*, for *by now*, is probably unnecessary.)

career industry. Any industry that affords to the workers an employment that will last for their working lives—hence, reasonable expectations of promotion. The everyday English would be *permanent job* or even *good job*.

carryback. First occurring in the U.S. Revenue Act of 1942, the term—which, for awkwardness, should be compared with *down-turn* and *rollback*—means 'an authorization to a taxpayer to recompute past taxes by carrying back specified deductions' (Funk and Wagnall's *New Standard Encyclopedia Year Book for* 1943).

case. 'Avoid *case* whenever you can' is sound advice. For instance, *in this case, in that case* usually=here, there; *in the case of*, as in 'In the case of unforeseen circumstances, the Heads of Department will act promptly and as seems fit' (In a contingency, the Heads . . .), usually=*in* or *on*, *for* or *about*. Or the sentence can be turned, as 'Q' turned 'In the case of John Jenkins deceased, the coffin provided, was of the usual character' (cf. **character**) into 'John Jenkins's coffin . . .' and commented, 'Coffins have no character, usual or unusual'; he probably re-wrote the sentence thus, 'John Jenkins's coffin was the usual kind'. He described *case* as 'Jargon's dearest child'.

Many other guardians of English have spoken contemptuously of officials' and journalists' illicit passion for this singularly risible word: yet these officials and journalists go on using it, as in 'The Ministry of Food receives more complaints than is the case of the Ministry of Transport' (The M. of F. receives more complaints than the M. of T.) and 'In the case of John Doc, we know what he has suffered' (We know what John Doc has suffered).

See also the separate entry **in the case of.**

casus belli. A *cause*, or *occasion*, *of war;* an event, officially called an *incident*, that serves as a *pretext of war*.

categorize, category—recategorize, recategorization. To class or classify; a class or division—reclassify; reclassification.

The extraordinary preference by officials (whether of the combatant Services or of the Civil Service) of *category* to *class* (or *division*) forms one of most easily recognizable features of jargon. The noun being so popular, the verb soon followed; that verb leads to *re-categorize;* it is unthinkable that so noble a verb should lack a noun—hence, the monstrosity *recategorization* (separate entry).

cause to be informed. 'The Minister desires that his staff will cause all applicants to be informed that the vacancies no longer exist'=The staff will tell applicants that the positions (or jobs) have been filled.

ceiling; ceiling price. Strictly, *ceiling*, a maximum price, the highest price, is elliptical for *ceiling price;* and in *ceiling price*, *ceiling* originally denoted 'limit', especially a limit fixed by governmental decree. In this larger sense, *ceiling* has persisted. But there seems to be no good reason why *ceiling* should have been invested with the meanings so satisfactorily associated with the nouns *limit* and *maximum* and with the adjectives *highest*, *utmost*, and—if it must be used—*maximum*. 'A new ceiling in exports.'

century storage. Such a storage of commodities as will ensure a continuance of supplies during a period when supplies are scarce. Why not *adequate storage?* Here we have, not polysyllabic excess but the use of the grossly exaggerative term, *century*.

channelize, channelization (America). See **canalize.**

character, for 'sort, kind', and especially *of a* (for instance, *dangerous*) *character* for a simple adjective (e.g. *dangerous*), has been vigorously attacked both by Sir Arthur Quiller-Couch in 1913 and by Sir Ernest Gowers in 1948. The latter quotes 'These claims are of a very far-reaching character'=These claims are very far-reaching. Compare the quotation at **nature.**

characterize; be characterized by. Usually this woolliness can be avoided by a sane use of either *have* or, if the context demands it, *possess*, or again by *show* or *display*. Thus: 'The proposal is characterized by a gross disregard of common decency'=The proposal shows a gross . . .'; 'Carelessness characterizes this memorandum'=This memorandum is careless; 'No merit at all characterizes the suggestion'=The suggestion has no merit, or The suggestion lacks—or, entirely lacks—merit.

circumstances. See **in the present circumstances.**

civilianisation (or **-ization**). Conversion of a garrison town, or of any other military centre, into a commercial town or other civilian centre. Occurring in a White Paper issued early in December 1951.

clarify and its noun **clarification** have, in official circles, long supplanted 'to *clear*' (or, *clear up*)', a *clearing*(*-up*), or 'to *explain*', *explanation*. Nowadays Whitehall 'clarifies a political, or a financial, situation'. This pair has also invaded academic jargon, as in 'In this section we are concerned with offering the reader opportunities for clarifying the human associations that radiate in intricate diversity from his preoccupation with himself as an individual. But this clarification of the nature of human experience . . .': Edward A. Post, 'Social Values', in *Essays in Value*, edited by Irving White (New York 1938).

To *clarify a problem*, political, economic, social, rarely=to solve it; usually it=to talk learnedly about it; to expound it.

classified into the following classes. Classified thus or, in some few instances, arranged in the following classes. Such tautology would, of course, horrify all those Civil Servants who have been tolerably educated; too many officers in Local Government lack education.

cognizance of, take. To notice; especially, to heed. 'It would be advisable to take cognizance of the mass of information presented for your attention.'

coincident with. (Mostly American.) During.

combat fatigue; combat neurosis. The former is probably a euphemism for the latter. Both are American terms, as are the synonymous *war fatigue* and the more technical *operational fatigue.* They all mean 'strain—especially, nervous strain—caused by active service' and they cover a larger class of symptoms than the outmoded yet effective *shell-shock.*

commence; in the commencement. To *begin,* (occasionally) to *start; in the beginning* or, more briefly, *at first*— or, if the context precludes *at first,* perhaps *originally.*

See especially Fowler's *Modern English Usage.*

communicate, to pass (in writing), to write; to tell. Hence, *communication,* a letter, a note; (a piece of) information. 'We shall communicate with you further if and when the occasion arises'=If necessary, we shall write to you again.

Probably adopted from commercialese.

comparatively, like **relatively,** is often used by Civil Servants (and others) when comparison has been neither stated nor even implied. See the quotation at **relatively.**

comprised of. Composed of.

conceptual, as used in analytical psychology and in metaphysics, is faultless; applied by Whitehall and Washington to political and Civil Service matters, it becomes decidedly faulty. Compare the reference at **ratiocination.**

concerning. *About,* as in 'Concerning the recent pronouncement . . .'; *on,* as in 'Concerning the ancient laws of Ruritania, the Minister very properly thinks that there exists no greater authority than himself'. Compare **relating to** and **vis à vis.**

conclusion emerges that, the. (For *a conclusion to which all of us would readily assent,* see **consideration . . .;** variant: *a conclusion with which the majority,* or *most of us, would agree.*) I, we, conclude that, or deduce that; often an adverb (e.g.

finally) or an adverbial phrase (e.g. *in short*) or a conjunction (*therefore* or *then*) would be better than the pompous *the conclusion emerges that . . .*

condition, noun. Like **character** and **nature, order** and **degree,** the noun *condition* has led, or incited, mankind to much official and other verbosity. 'Q' indicted it thus: '*Condition.* He was conveyed to his place of residence in an intoxicated condition. "He was carried home drunk." '

Under present conditions and *conditions being what they are* mean *at present* or *now*. Has *now* caught the plague?

condition, verb. To shape or mould; to determine; to control —or, rather, to tend to control or be designed to control; to train. 'The strange and often terrible circumstances of "the London Blitz" have unpredictably conditioned the character of many a Londoner.' Often the word required is simply 'to *change*', as in 'The Minister's decision to act promptly has conditioned his whole outlook'.

[**conflagration.** A fire. This pomposity is not peculiar to officialese.]

connection (or **connexion**) **with, in.** See **in connection . . .**

conservative estimate. A moderate or restrained or sensible estimate.

consider. To think; to believe; to hold (the opinion). In these nuances, *consider* is not merely officialese: it is a catachresis or, less learnedly, a misuse. *Consider* properly means 'to think about, to think over, to weigh, to deliberate the potentialities of'.

considerable is one of those vague and sonorous adjectives of intensification which are far too popular among officials. 'This is a matter of considerable importance' =This matter is important; or, This is important.

Compare **substantial.**

consideration; considerations. 'Tags like *a consideration which we should do well to bear in mind* or *a conclusion to which* *all of us would readily assent* will save many a sentence from coming down with a bump,' George Orwell.

Compare 'We should bear in mind the following considerations: (1) . . . ; (2) . . . ; (3) . . . ': for which, substitute *Points to note* (not *to be noted*)—and then state the points.

consolidate, consolidation. To summarize, to précis (e.g. a report); to incorporate (one piece of evidence in a body of evidence); to combine or unite. Both the summary and the collective evidence afford examples of **consolidation.** (For the verb, as for the noun, the 'summary' or 'abstract' or 'précis' nuance is the commoner.) This began by being Services' jargon; unfortunately the virus has spread.

consume, to eat, ranks among ordinary people as a genteelism; for some, it seems to achieve elegance. For the official—rather the Local Government officer than the true Civil Servant—it has more dignity than *eat* and has therefore supplanted it.

content, in the sense 'the amount (of some specified matter or material) contained in, or yielded by that which contains it', as in 'the vitamin content of bread' or 'the tar content of coal', is being grossly overworked in Government offices, where *high protein contents* and *low vitamin contents* and even *the education content* (of, e.g. a book) are comforting verbal counters.

conurbation. Outlying towns that have coalesced with a city—e.g. London or Chicago—to form a loosely knit community, at least for such purposes as traffic regulations or defence. Only once in his attack upon official jargon, was Norman Riley unfair: it concerned this odd-looking, yet occasionally unavoidable *conurbation.* (See the quotation at **demonstratee.**)

co-ordinated plan; co-ordination. In *a co-ordinated plan,* the *co-ordinated* is unnecessary: a plan implies co-ordination, otherwise it is, strictly, not a plan at all. As Sir Alan Herbert, in *What a Word!* (1935), trenchantly remarked, 'We no longer work together: we co-operate according to a co-ordinated plan'.

For *co-ordination*, compare the quotation at **panel discussion.** Often, it is a good word, a necessary word; too often, it means no more than *arrangement* or *plan.*

correspondence. Letters.

coverage. Extent, scope; hence, protection. This Americanism, which is creeping into British official jargon and British journalese, has been brilliantly 'covered' in *The New Yorker's* picture (August 4, 1951) of a young 'stuffed shirt' proposing to a girl, thus: 'With me, Mabel, you would always enjoy the comfort of security. I have an ample base salary with a cost-of-living escalator arrangement, group life insurance, and full Blue Cross coverage' and more to the same impassioned tune. For another unpleasant word in *-age*, compare **overage.**

create. To *establish* a governmental department or a branch or section of one.

critical components. Essential parts of very important war machines (e.g. aircraft); hence, since August 1945, essential parts of all very important machines. Originally and still mainly an American term.

cubicalize (or **-ise**): To convert a hall, a (large) room, into cubicles; to make cubicles the predominant feature of (a building, a hospital); to put (patients) into cubicles; to convert (a school) from the dormitory to the cubicle system. I had not seen this horrible word until I read Norman Riley's 'Dehydrated English'.

customer-resistance. A misleading and unnecessary variation of the better-known *sales-resistance*. How unnecessary it is will appear quite damningly from the quotation made at **over-availability.**

cutback. A drastic reduction in raw materials or in goods—a reduction caused by a suddenly diminished demand, as, for example, in the materials, etc., required by an army. In form, comparable to **carryback, down-turn** and, especially, **rollback.**

D

data. Facts; information. In gobbledygook, *data* is always a singular noun, as in 'The data set forth in this document is unconvincing'. Compare **datum . . .**

date as postmark. Although so common in letters from officials, this heading never ceases to astonish me. It is discourteous: and discourtesy has not yet become a predominant characteristic of Civil Servants. For filing and other purposes of reference, it must cause many a clerk a splitting headache.

datum line; datum point. 'One mining crisis, I remember'—that was in 1935—'raged for months round something called the *datum* line,' Sir Alan Herbert. Then there are *datum point* and *datum level* (or *plane*). Officialese is bad enough without these technicalities being sneaked into it.

de-. 'A. P. H.' has called the official passion for verbs (and their derivative nouns) in *de-* the 'de-fever'. He quotes such abominations as 'methods of dehumidifying the air' and *de-insectization.*

Compare the entry at **re-de.**

deadline. Any fixed limit—whether a *starting-point* (or *-time*) or a *terminus*, an *ultimate point* or a *latest time.* See especially *Webster's*, in the main body of the dictionary, and, for its adoption into Britain, Sir Ernest Gowers, *ABC of Plain Words.*

debrief. (American.) To instruct passengers before they land at an airport in what is required of them by Customs and the Passport Office and in what they have to do about getting to their further destination. Cf. **brief.**

decided, it has been—occasionally, **it is.** 'It has ultimately been decided by the competent authorities that the clarification proposed by Mr X be accepted'=Mr X's clarification has at last been accepted.

[**decimate,** to destroy a large number or part of, is not officialese: it is merely loose English.]

decontaminate. To cleanse; to rid or clear of gas. *Decontamination*, a cleansing—or cleansing as a process. Compare, at **re-de,** their horrendous offspring, *redecontaminate* and *redecontamination.*

de-control, verb and noun; **de-controlled,** adjective. (Compare **liberalize, liberalization.**) To end governmental control of, especially, a trade or a commodity; an ending of that control.

Norman Riley has satirized the term in the imaginary yet far too likely phrase, 'non-unrestricted de-control'.

de facto. In the fact; in fact; in reality. Contrast **de jure.** These Latin phrases belong to the lawyers.

definite, definitely. The intrusion, into officialese, of the almost meaningless use of *definite* and especially of *definitely* is deplorable. It should be left to those who have an irresistible longing to say nothing in as many words as they can muster.

Sir Ernest Gowers (*Plain Words*, p. 39), like Sir Alan Herbert before him, has some trenchant things to say about the maddeningly superfluous use of *definite* and *definitely.*

degree. '*Degree.* A singular degree of rarity prevails in the earlier editions of this romance.

'This is Jargon. In prose it runs simply "The earlier editions of this romance are rare"—or "are very rare",' Sir Arthur Quiller-Couch, 'Interlude: On Jargon', in *On the Art of Writing*, 1916.

'The building has suffered to a disastrous degree'=it has suffered disastrously.

dehydrate; dehydrated. To *dehydrate*, to free (fruit, vegetables) of water, may be all very well as a scientific or technological term: to market *dried fruits*, *dried vegetables*, as *dehydrated fruits* or *dehydrated vegetables* is to commit three crimes against English, the first being the substitution of a learned, little-known word for an everyday word, the second being to use a long word where a short one would serve equally well, or better, and the third being to prostitute a good word to the base uses of economists.

dehydrofreezing. This American term, which arose in 1946, means 'in the preservation of food, a method whereby the foods are partly dehydrated and then very quickly frozen'. (Modified from the definition in the New Words section of the *Britannica Book of the Year*, 1949.)

disinsecticize (or **-ise**); with derivative noun, **deinsecticization;** 'preferable' verb, **de-insectize,** 'preferable' noun, **deinsectization.** To rid (a place, a house, a room) of insects. When I saw the longer verb included in a list of terms indicted by Norman Riley, I felt sceptical. I had forgotten Sir Alan Herbert's attack on the 'preferable' noun, sixteen years earlier, in *What a Word!* Both forms of the verb and the noun revolt every right-minded person. Cf. **de-ratization.**

de jure. By right; by lawful title. Contrast **de facto**—and then decide to renounce both of them.

delimit and **demarcate; delimitation, demarcation.** 'A frontier is not "defined", nor "fixed", nor even "determined", but "delimited" or "demarcated",' Sir Alan Herbert in 1935. The fear he expresses in 'And it will not be much longer, I suppose, before it is "delimitated"' had been realized before he expressed it: *Webster* (1934) has '*delimitate* . . . To delimit'.

Demarcation, the act of distinguishing or delimiting, is also employed by officialese for things other than frontiers.

demarcate, demarcation. See **delimit.**

demise, permissible in Law, is abominable outside it; more, it is as inept as it is unnecessary; and it is completely unnecessary.

demonstrate. 'Of the ordinary, blunt English words we all understand, a place is now a "conurbation"; a chimney-sweep a "flueologist"; a rat-catcher a "rodent operator"; a rise in prices an "upward adjustment"; a hopeful customer for a new car a "demonstratee"; and a reasonable appetite a "minimum calory intake",' Norman Riley, in his delectable 'Dehydrated English'. As *lessee* to *lessor*, so (one supposes) *demonstratee* to *demonstrator*. Ugh! Even the insurance man's *prospect* is better than *demonstratee*.

de-nationalize and its noun, **de-nationalization.** To restore to its private owners an industry or other activity (e.g. an air line) that has been *nationalized*, i.e. taken over by the State. See **nationalize.**

depth interview. A long, comprehensive, searching interview in which a psychiatrist tries to get at the subject's subconscious. Adopted by Army and other psychiatrists and professional interviewers. Apparently coined, 1948, in America.

de-ratize, deratization; or **-ise, -isation.** To kill rats; especially, to rid (a place, a building) of rats. In *What a Word!* Sir Alan Herbert mentioned it with scorn, as he did the noun *de-ratization;* in 1940 Dr Hubert Jagger (*English in the Future*) pointed out the noun, only to add that he thought it would soon die; but in 1951—witness Norman Riley—it still flourished. Perhaps the rodent operator is less efficient than the old *rat-catcher*.

derequisition. To *free* (a property, especially a building); the connotation being: 'from government control'; but, to avoid confusion with the next term, I recommend 'to *restore*'—i.e. a property to its rightful occupants.

de-restricted; de-restriction. 'Was it necessary . . . to add the word "Derestriction" to our language in order to say that the speed-limit would no longer be enforced on certain roads? Would not "exemption" or "liberation" have served as well and sounded better?': Sir Alan Herbert, 1935.

I should, if I were asked, propose 'to *free*' and 'a *freeing*'.

deserving of serious consideration. In officialese, George Orwell once remarked, 'the ends of sentences are saved from anticlimax by such resounding commonplaces as *greatly to be desired, cannot be left out of account, . . . deserving of serious consideration* . . . and so on and so forth'.

In short, *important.*

description. 'The project is of a visionary description'=The plan will not work; or, The plan is impractical. For *description,* the official padder could—and often does—substitute *character* or *nature.*

Compare **character, condition, nature, order.**

desiderate; desideratum (plural, **desiderata**). 'We say not "What is wanted is . . ." but "The requisites desiderated consist in" . . .,' Sir Alan Herbert, 1935. (Note that *requisites desiderated* is tautological for either *requisites* or *desiderata.*)

Both *desiderate* and *desideratum,* anything lacking, anything desired or demanded as an essential, were literary and learned words before they passed to the upper reaches of officialdom.

desirous that, be. *To be*—or *to be at present—desirous that,* for *desire,* or, better, to *wish,* belongs as much to commercialese as to officialese.

desterilize (Noun: **desterilization.**) To return, e.g. 'frozen' money, to useful service, 'as gold from an insulated condition in the treasury to use as a basis for [the issuing of] additional currency certificates' (*Webster*).

Gold is *sterilized* when the Treasury renders it (temporarily) unusable; that state is officially known as *sterilization.* Although objectionable, this sense is at least preferable to the lunacy recorded at **sterilize.**

determine. To decide; to ordain. 'It has been determined that the plan shall be put into operation on the night of the 20th.' For an American example, see the quotation at **panel discussion.** As used in official jargon, *determine* often means no more than to *appoint, arrange, fix* (a date, especially that of a meeting).

de-trunk. (Not, please notice, *detrunk,* obsolete for *detruncate,* to shorten by cutting, to decapitate.) To convert a telephone exchange on trunk call into an exchange requiring only a local call; to render an exchange no longer available, even by trunk call, to another. Also, to declare a trunk road no longer a trunk road or, especially, to lessen its traffic and therefore its importance.

develop; development. '*Develop* blocks the way to the preferable *happen, occur, take place* and *come* or *come about,*' Sir Ernest Gowers, who later adds *grow. Development,* therefore, is, by officials, made to supersede *happening, occurrence, growth.* A further official sense of develop is 'to arise', as in 'An unforeseen difficulty has developed'.

deviation, deviationism, devationist. These three terms, belonging to the jargon of communism, have been adopted by bureaucracy and the press. A *deviationist* is anyone guilty of *deviationism,* and the abstract collective noun *deviationism* signifies all *deviations* or swervings from communist theory and practice and all failures to obey the Communist Party's directives.

devoid of, be. To lack. 'The Uptopian emissary would appear to be devoid of sympathy for our nation' = The Utopian emissary lacks sympathy . . . = has no time for us.

devolution. A passing or transference or delegation, especially of powers, rights, privileges, property. *Devolution for Scotland* = a separate government—or, independence—for Scotland.

devolve upon. To fall to or (up)on. 'After the Governor's death, responsibility inevitably devolved upon his inexperienced deputy.'

dichotomy, a technicality of logic and astronomy, biology and botany, means predominantly '(a system of) division, and subdivision, by two'. Federal prose has adopted and adapted the word. Mr Paul R. Porter, head of E.C.A., has objected to the word being used by his staff. (Report in the New York *Herald Tribune* of October 14, 1951.)

dietary; dietary standard. Already in 1935 Sir Alan Herbert could lament that 'You will read about one "diet" now for ten "dietaries".' Since then, we have had inflicted upon us something known as *dietary standards*, defined in the 1949 *Funk and Wagnalls* as 'the kinds and amounts of food needed to provide a stated number of calories per day per person'. (This use of *per* itself belongs to officialese.)

dilutee. Industrial—but also Civil Service—jargon for an unskilled worker added to a staff of skilled workers.

directive. In the *New York World Telegram* of April 6, 1946 Frank Aston objected to the use of the word. It had occurred, in its military sense, as early as 1934 in *Webster's*. This military sense, 'general orders—coming from a supreme headquarters or, at least, from an army headquarters—setting forth the general lines of a campaign or of a very important single operation', ranks as Service jargon. The word becomes questionable when it is made to apply to a mere administrative order and thoroughly objectionable when it denotes an unimportant regulation.

dis-. The abuse of *dis-*, eloquently deplored by Sir Alan Herbert in *What a Word!* (pp. 29-30), is seen to its best disadvantage in the ensuing terms: **disassemble, disequilibrium, disincentive, dis-saver.**

disassemble. 'To "disassemble" (an engine), beloved by certain low fellows in the motor-trade. What a wicked word! Dis-assemble! The engineers of our glorious Navy say "strip an engine"—swift and metaphorical and true. That should be good enough for any motor-monger ashore,' A. P. Herbert, *What a Word!* (1935). The opposite to '*as*semble' is '*dis*semble': but *dissemble* would lead to ambiguity.

discontinue. Officialese does not say 'Please stop that!', nor even 'We ask you to cease doing that', but 'We request that this'—or 'the present'—'practice be discontinued'. Compare the quotation at **substitution** and, for **discontinuance** (a closing), at **scheduled for discontinuance.**

disequilibrium. For a painful example, see the quotation at **underdelivery.** Norman Riley has told us, very politely by implication, what he thinks of it. Sir Alan Herbert, in 1935, permitted himself this mild pronouncement: 'Now, "equilibrium" is an exact word . . .; to add "dis-" 'to it does not make another exact word but a vague and feeble word. I like "disequilibrium" as little as I should like "disabsolutely" for "not quite" or "disunique" for "common" '. Besides, it's a pompous word.

disincentive. In the *Britannica Book of the Year* 1950, J. M. Wyllie defines it as 'a deterrent, especially to patriotic behaviour'; by late 1951 it was more often used to denote a deterrent to wholehearted work, as though, for many, their own characters did not already form a sufficient deterrent. See also the reference at **ratiocination.**

disparity. Inequality; difference.

disposition. This word becomes objectionable in the verbose *of a* (so-and-so) *disposition* used instead of a simple adjective. 'He is of an amiable disposition'='He is amiable'. Sir Ernest Gowers aligns it with such words as **character, description, nature;** it stands on a par with Sir Arthur Quiller-Couch's **condition.**

dis-saver. One who, instead of saving more money, saves less; the tendency, like the practice, is *dis-saving*. 'Politicians have added "dissavers" to the glowing vocabulary of modern economics' (Norman Riley).

distribution of industrial policy. Economese for 'such governmental control over new factories as will prevent mass unemployment in the districts in which the factories arise'. (Sir Ernest Gowers, *ABC*, p. 76.)

divulge, to disclose, is basically an elegancy, common to all lovers or slaves of the genteel; yet it has a certain dignity: and that dignity has won for it a warm place in the departmental affections of our officials.

domicile, noun; **be domiciled at.** Comparable to **divulge** is *domicile*, which, as a legal technicality, will pass but which, as a variation upon the theme of *house* or *home*, just won't do. *To be domiciled at*, dear to the police and formerly to the staff of Inland Revenue, is still worse; to *dwell*, more familiarly to *live*, should be good enough for anybody.

donate, for 'to *give*', is one of those 'snob-words' (Sir Alan Herbert's description) which have meretriciously seduced Whitehall from its purity and sedateness. Sir Alan lists under that heading the following terms I have included in this glossary: **advise, commence, envisage, ideology, measure, rendition, versed.**

down-turn. A *decrease* in output, a *slackening* or *falling-off* in work, a *reduction* of subsidies, a *lessening* of, or *loss* in, the national income. But in what respect is *down-turn* superior to any of those six synonyms? Perhaps the lure of 'on the *down*-grade' proved too much for some neologically-minded bureaucrat seeking a cheap reputation. *Down-turn* is ugly to look at and ugly to say.

due date, at the. See **at the . . .**

duly noted is a frequent officialism for *noted*. 'Your request has been duly noted.'

duplex, adjective. Double. Commoner in the United States than in Britain.

E

economic independence. A fair living. *To attain economic independence* is, for an individual, *to make a living* or—not a popular ideal, this—*to earn all one needs* or, specifically, *to earn enough money to be able to do without State assistance.*

edible fat. A cooking fat. Why substitute the inaccurate *edible* for the accurate *cooking?* Compare the quotation at **non-.**

educationist or **educator.** (American.) A teacher.

effect. To do. Compare:

effect a change—a reduction—a saving, etc. To *make a change*, etc.; occasionally, to *change, reduce, save.* Especially, **effect a radical alteration**=to *alter*, or *change*, things *considerably* or *very much.*

effectuate, effectuation. In 1935 Sir Alan Herbert quoted, from Western Australia's petition to the British Parliament, the words, 'to effectuate the restoration of Western Australia to its former status' (one need not, after that, wonder why W. A. didn't get political independence), and, from a Service periodical, the equally barbarous 'effectuation of this purpose'.

Better: to *effect.* Better still: to *accomplish,* with noun *accomplishment.*

elemental. Fundamental; primary. Rather an American than a British piece of officialese.

elements. (The singular is rare.) In *Usage and Abusage* Eric Partridge quotes *The Star* (London): 'The Central News reports that unrest prevailed among certain "military and political elements". The elements, it was added, were being energetically suppressed': that is, soldiers and politicians were being either shot to death or, in a concentration camp, buried for life. It is odd, how often the accompanying adjective is *dangerous* (as in the *Daily Mail*, August 13, 1951)—when it isn't *subversive.*

emanate from. To *proceed* or *issue* from; loosely, to result or come from. An elegancy adopted by many officials. In many ways it is on a level with **transpire;** yet, on the whole, it isn't quite so bad as that horror.

employ of, be in the. To be employed by; better to work for. Regarded by some officials as a genteel expression.

enclosed herewith. A tautology adored by officials. *Enclosed* would suffice. Compare:

enclosed please find (a remittance for . . .). Commercialese, adopted by officials. Sir Ernest Gowers awards it a very black mark.

endeavour, verb. To try. Then there is the partly commercialese, partly official verbosity of *it will be our endeavour to* (do something): after which, usually nothing is done.

enquire. See **inquire.**

entail, verb. To cause (for someone); to impose. 'The enactment of this regulation will entail much careful planning' = To carry out this regulation, we must plan carefully. Adopted from legal phraseology.

entertainment(-)value. 'To-day, instead of "fun", we learn to speak of "entertainment-value"; instead of Tories we have "the forces of reaction"; instead of games, "recreational facilities" ' (A. P. Herbert, *What a Word!*, 1935): and so lose much of the fun.

entities. See **entity.**

entitlement. This piece of jargon occurs more frequently perhaps in the Services than in the other governmental professions. In general, it means *rights* or (a) *right;* less vaguely, *moneys;* more particularly, an *allowance*—or a *share* or *issue* due *to* someone ('His entitlement is 27s per week').

entity. (Rare in the singular.) *Entities*: things. Much commoner in North America than in Britain.

entrance permit. (American.) A pass.

envisage. To face; to contemplate; to plan or, rather, to have in mind. 'The Minister does not envisage so drastic a measure'=The Minister plans something less severe.

equally as. Whether it means 'equally', as usually it does, or 'as much as', *equally as* is a misuse; the former, tautological, and the latter, illiterate. I should not have included this catachresis, were it not that, during 1950-51, I espied it, perhaps half a dozen times, in official writings.

erratum; plural, **errata.** An error in manuscript or typescript or print; an author's or a printer's error. Among scholars, *errata* (or *corrigenda*) may be all right; both for laymen, whom it is (theoretically) the business of Civil Servants to serve, and for the increasingly large number of only partly literate Local Government clerks, well-educated officials would be wise to write *printer's* (or *printers'*) *errors* or, where printers are not concerned, *errors*.

escalation, escalator. (Compare thc quotation at **coverage.**) From that *escalator clause* which deals with *escalation* or the right to increase tonnage—a '*scaling up*', as it were—comes the modern sense: such a clause in a contract as allows for a rise or fall in prices or wages, according to the tendency observable in prices, wages and, especially, the cost of living.

essential; it is essential that. As Sir Ernest Gowers has enjoined upon Civil Servants less adept than himself, *essential* is a strong word and is therefore exposed to over-work. 'It is essential that you remember to avoid offending a people only too easy to offend': you would be well-advised to avoid . . .

essentialize. To ascertain, or to state, the essentials of; to reduce (something) to its essentials or to its essence. Although 'in character', *essentialize* has not much caught the official fancy; only the literary and perhaps the analysts use it.

evacuate, evacuation; evacuee. To send—the sending of—civilians from an area threatened with plague or gas or, especially, aerial bombing, to a safe or, at least, a safer area; the persons sent are *evacuees*. This is an official development of the 1914-1918 official sense 'to send ill or wounded troops home from the firing line or from the hospitals'. To *remove*, with noun *removal*, would have served the purpose; and, for *evacuee*, we could have used *those removed*.

eventuality; eventuate. An *event;* especially, a *possibility* borne in mind. To *eventuate* means 'to *happen*, to *occur*, to *come to pass*'. Sir Alan Herbert quotes from Sir Stafford Cripps, serious devotee of jargon, the revealing words, 'Then Mr Baldwin must show us that it was necessary in any grouping that might eventuate'=Then Mr Baldwin must prove that, whatever the grouping, it was necessary.

evince. To show, as in 'He evinced courage of the highest sort'. Among inexperienced journalists as well as among would-be elegant officials the word is a favourite. By 1945, I'd say, it had also become rather old-fashioned, an outdated genteelism.

ex gratia payment. A payment made, not by legal necessity but as a favour; a payment made in (tacit) recognition of a moral obligation. Perhaps *ex gratia payment* is a necessary evil; certainly *ex gratia* by itself is no longer permissible to good writers and should be eschewed by right-minded officials.

exhibit a tendency to. To incline or tend to; to be seen to. 'He exhibits a tendency to belittle all his competitors.' That is verbose and pompous.

Merely pompous is the continual use of *exhibit* for 'to show'—compare the quotation at *malnutrition*.

expend. To spend; to pay. 'Any sum expended for the purpose of providing a site for a school' = any sum paid to buy a school site.

explore. To investigate (a problem). Compare the political cliché, **to explore every avenue.**

extend. To *make* (a food that is either scarce or expensive) *go further* by adding, usually at the preparatory stage, a more plentiful or a cheaper food, as in 'to extend meat with cereal' (1944 *Britannica Book of the Year*). This seems to be a specialized nuance of the sense defined by *Webster's* as 'to increase in quantity by admixture; as, to extend liquors by weakening or adulterating them'. The added 'inferior' element is known as the *extender.*

Contrast **restore.**

F

facilitate, facilitation; affirmative facilitation. To make easy—especially, to make easier; a making easy or easier. Of *affirmative facilitation*, Peter Edson, newspaper writer, supplies us with an example. Referring to the governmental pamphlet, *Business and Government* (published late in 1949), he says that the President's Council of Economic Advisers 'would rather talk about "affirmative facilitation", as this report does, instead of just "make things easier"'. Mr Edson's article, entitled 'Tops in Gobbledygook', affords some alarming instances of Federal prose.

factor has become a general-utility word, vague and often disconcerting. It has too often displaced *fact, consideration—causation, cause—circumstance, occurrence, happening—feature,* or *characteristic—element, constituent.* Admittedly this misuse is not confined to officials, but officials do very often fall into it; Sir Ernest Gowers has included *factor* in his list of 'words that are overworked in official documents'. (See especially Eric Partridge, *Usage and Abusage*, p. 115 of the British edition.)

fact that, the. Because. 'The fact that the Minister has graciously accorded an interview is not to be interpreted as being tantamount to the granting of your request.' George Orwell has included *the fact that* in his list of long-winded substitutes for simple conjunctions.

feasible. ' "Feasible," Bobby, means "doable", not "possible", "probable," or "likely". A revolution might be feasible tomorrow, but not rain,' Sir Alan Herbert, *What a Word!*

(p. 107). Yet how often we hear Ministers of State, Civil Servants and other officials speaking of things being—usually, not being—*feasible* when they mean 'possible', or 'impossible', and when, by using this wrong word, they are being disconcertingly ambiguous.

feather-bedding (or one word) is the euphemism that conceals the effectual operation of Trade Union rules—*featherbed rules*—for limiting the amount of work to be done or of goods to be produced, a limitation imposed in order to make jobs last longer and thus prevent or, at the least, diminish unemployment. Recourse to *Webster's* leads one to suppose a sense-development from American railwaymen's slang.

[**Federal prose.** See Introduction.]

feeding-point. 'Earlier this year,' writes an anonymous critic in the *Evening Standard*, August 17, 1951, 'the Festival of Britain Office introduced a new horror of its own construction by talking about "feeding-points", a clumsy euphemism for canteens and tea-trolleys. It ranked with the Ministry of Health's classic "accommodation unit" [? a room], which Mr Churchill killed stone-dead by singing the phrase to the tune of Home, Sweet Home.'

field. (Mostly American.) One's subject or profession. 'The teaching field is understaffed'—quoted by Masterson & Phillips. Presumably from such scientific contexts as 'the magnetic field'.

filed for future reference. Usually this official tag means no more than that your letter has been received, or that your request has (you hope) been read, but probably will be referred-to never again. Why not simply 'Your letter has been filed'?

finalize—finalization. To end or stop (something); to conclude; to bring it to an end or a conclusion, to terminate.

The noun has been pilloried in Norman Riley's 'the finalisation of the day'. The verb has been attacked by Sir Alan Herbert, Eric Partridge, Sir Ernest Gowers, Norman Riley, and others; yet certain Civil Servants and many Local Government Authorities persist in using it and (what is so pathetic) being rather proud of familiarity with this noisome creature.

finances. Money—especially the government's. Compare **funds.**

firm containment. 'The keeping of a nation within its boundaries by means of firm opposition' (*Britannica* year-book published in 1949).

flueologist, chimney-sweep, ranks with *rodent operator* for inverted snobbery and for seemingly learned stupidity; and with *charlady* for a risibly ill-placed euphemism. Both *flueologist* and *rodent operator* have been salutarily castigated by Norman Riley. (See the quotation at **demonstratee.**)

following. Sir Alan Herbert, Eric Partridge and Sir Ernest Gowers have shown how horrible can be the use of *following* for the simple and unambiguous *after*, as in 'Following our recent warning, our instructions on the subject are as follows', or 'You are hereby advised to disclose all the sources of your income, following the fact that you are now well known to be a successful inventor'. But perhaps the fiercest attack is that made by G. V. Carey in his excellent handbook on punctuation: *Mind the Stop!* Compare the quotation at **subsequent to.**

forces of reaction, the. General, not specifically official, jargon for conservatism, Conservatives, Tories. See the quotation at **entertainment value.**

forecast of future needs. Forecast of needs; estimated needs.

for the purpose of (doing something). In order to; to (do something). For a good example, see the quotation at **expend.**

for your information is, ninety-nine times out of a hundred, superfluous. 'For your information, I have been directed to state that the goods have not yet become available'=The goods are not ready.

found that, if it be; it will (or **may**) **be found that.** *If you find that* is preferable to *if it be* (or *is*) *found that*, yet very often *if* will do the work required; likewise, *you will* (or *may*) *find that* is preferable to the passive form, but for the *may* variation, a simple *perhaps* will do the trick. The next time you see, or detect yourself writing . . . *be found that*, please examine it for yourself.

foundation, adjective. In the United States, at least among officials, it has displaced *fundamental*. Thus, 'The basic elements; the foundation principles' (Masterson and Phillips).

fringe wage. (American.) Such wages as, if they were raised, would not add much to the cost of production. A War Labor Board term.

from every angle. Entirely; in every way; in every respect. Ponder the example quoted by Sir Ernest Gowers: 'Bare boards are unsatisfactory from every angle'; an example clearly exposed to ribald comment. Compare:

from the standpoint—viewpoint or, preferably, **point of view—angle—of.** 'From the standpoint (or viewpoint or angle) of the ultimate destination of these "top secret" goods, it would be well to bear in mind also their possible value to the enemy if he should capture them'=Before despatching these goods, we must guard against their falling into the enemy's hands.

function, noun. Especially in (one's) **function as** or **of.** '*Function* should be substituted for *duty, habit, characteristic, operation*, or any other word about which the writer is in doubt' (Masterson and Phillips, ironically).

function, verb intransitive. To work; to act. 'The machine functions imperfectly'; 'The new Department, it is hoped, will function no less efficiently than the old'; 'Although a makeshift, this device should function satisfactorily' (*serve*, or *serve the purpose*).

functionalist. One who preaches—one who practises—usefulness and adaptability as the primary virtues in, e.g., architecture; his creed is *functionalism*. Both of these terms derive from *functional*, 'serving a useful purpose; subserving a specific activity or end'—in short, *practical*. Originally, American.

funds. Money. Compare **finances** and **units of currency.**

furnish particulars. To give or supply information; to state one's needs or purpose. 'If you will be so good as to furnish the necessary particulars . . .'=If you tell us what you want (or, propose) . . .

Adopted from commercialese.

further issue, a; no further issue. Any (or some) more; no more. 'Do not say . . . *I am sorry that I cannot at present consider a further issue* for *I am sorry that I cannot let you have any more at present*,' Sir Ernest Gowers, *Plain Words:* perhaps rather *I regret that I can allow you no more.*

future, in the (**very**) **near.** Why must officials keep on using this wordy phrase for (*very*) *soon* or, where *soon* does not provide the exact nuance, (*very*) *shortly?*

G

gainfully employed. See **lucrative employment.**

gear. To *modify* the production policy of a factory to accord with the needs of a group of factories or of an industrial organization.

give particular attention to; even—though much less objectionable—**attend particularly to.** To heed; to attend closely to. In 'We ask you to give particular attention to the set of instructions enclosed herewith', the precise meaning would be expressed better if *read carefully* were substituted for the offending phrase.

global. World-wide; comprehensive; *globally*: comprehensively or collectively or as a whole (as an entity). The nuance 'world-wide' is, in itself, permissible; but *global* has become the pet of officialdom, a Whitehall—and a Washington—vogue-word, often at the expense of terms much less ambiguous. (See, e.g., Sir Ernest Gowers, *op. cit.*, p. 53.)

[**gobbledygook.** 'Word coined by Maury Maverick to describe the involved and abstract language of Washington official documents. (1944.)': I. Willis Russell in *Britannica Book of the Year* 1945. Also see the Introduction.]

H

have a reasonable prospect—no prospect—of (doing something). To have, to see, a good chance—no chance—to do something.

have no alternative but, or **other than, to** (do something). To be forced or obliged to do something; to have to do it.

have the effect of. To result in; (in some contexts:) to resemble. This is one of those sonorous vacuities which that hard-hitter and straight-writer George Orwell damned as 'operators' or 'verbal false limbs'. Compare **militate against** and **render inoperative.**

having reference, or **regard, to.** About; in or on; for. 'Having reference to your communication of the 27th ult., the Minister desires me to . . .'

hereby, herein, hereto, heretofore, herewith. See **thereat . . .**

hiatus. A gap; an interval. Compare **interim.**

hive off. To pass to branches, or to subsidiary companies, the production not only of such goods as are about to become State-owned but also of those which, for the time being, are exempted from State-ownership, in order to prevent the parent, or the principal, company from becoming itself a State industry.

honoris causa; occasionally **honoris gratia.** A degree conferred *honoris causa*, for the sake of honour, i.e. honorifically, is permissible, for it is a university technicality. Outside that sphere, the phrase becomes pompous jargon.

hospitalize, hospitalization—occasionally **inhospitalization.** To *hospitalize* someone is to send (someone), or cause (him) to be sent, to hospital; the victim *is hospitalized;* the act, the process, the fact, are known as *hospitalization,* with the variant (British only) *inhospitalization.* These terms may have originated in the combatant services.

Hence, *hospitalization services,* such services as you might perhaps expect to receive in and from a hospital.

hypothesis, supposition; especially, **on the hypothesis that,** supposing. In jargon, as George Orwell pointed out in his famous article 'Politics and the English Language', 'simple conjunctions and prepositions are replaced by such phrases as *with respect to, having regard to, the fact that, by dint of, in the interests of, on the hypothesis that*'.

I

identify oneself with (e.g., a cause). To associate oneself with; to join; to support. In *What a Word!* (1935) Sir Alan Herbert quoted 'The past week has been a period of unparalleled jubilation, with which defendant and his fellow-countrymen have unreservedly identified themselves'. It was a Harley Street doctor who wrote that sentence; but *identify*, used thus, is characteristic of—indeed, an element in—officialese.

ideology, ideological. By Sir Alan Herbert, in 1935, stigmatized as a snob-word and, at that time, serving in so-called progressive circles as a synonym for 'a given person's principles and beliefs, or his attitude to life and politics', *ideology* and its derivatives *ideological* and *ideologist* have been translated to an ostensibly higher plane, as in this definition in the New Words section of *Webster:* 'The intellectual pattern of any widespread culture or movement . . .; specifically, the integrated assertions, theories, and aims constituting a politico-social program, often with an implication of factitious propagandizing.'

if and when. Either *if*—implying emphasis of the conditional—or *when*—emphasizing the time—will do the work. 'If and when the need arises, the Minister will decide' =If the need arise, the Minister will decide, *or* When the need arises, the Minister will decide.

impact. Effect; incidence; influence. 'The impact of sociology upon ignorance conduces to communism.'

impecunious is both a genteel elegancy and an obsolescent literarism for *poor;* it is also a word with which government officials have something more than a 'Good morning!' acquaintance.

[**impedimenta.** Baggage, luggage. This term is not yet one of the spoilt darlings or overworked employees of the bureaucrats; but I fear the worst.]

impermeabilize. To render (a material, an object) impermeable—i.e., impervious to liquid; especially, to *water-proof* it. This word affords us an unusually fine specimen of jargon gone mad.

implement; implementation. For a quotation of the latter (meaning 'fulfilment') see **panel discussion.**

To *implement*, to fulfil (a promise), to accomplish or carry out (a plan, an undertaking), was, in the 1920's and 1930's, a vogue word among intellectuals. The war relegated it to official circles: it has, for some time, been a favourite of the Civil Service. The modern sense may have arisen from the revival of interest in the works of Sir Walter Scott, who speaks of 'revenge . . . implemented by the hand of Vanbeest Brown'; incidentally, the term exists in Scots Law—to implement or fulfil (a contract).

in camera. Behind locked—or, at the least, closed and guarded—doors; in secret. 'The case was tried *in camera*' = privately.

incapacitated. See **by reason of.**

incentive bonus. A bonus *in advance* as an encouragement, for workers, to work. The newspapers of 15 September 1951 reported a flagrant example.

incentive pay. Increased pay for increased production; stakhanovitis, which operates at its healthiest in a piece-work system but which exemplifies a principle perhaps unhealthy—that of never doing any work that one isn't paid for. Lexicographically, a border-line case.

incident. See **casus belli.**

incident to. Connected with; arising from. 'Liquidation is incident to political intransigence.'

inclined to believe—to think—that. These 'cautionary clichés' (as Sir Ernest Gowers has neatly called them) mean very little or else mean something other than what they appear to mean: they don't mean 'I am moving towards a belief—the thought—that . . .'; they do, I fear, mean 'I believe—I think—but I haven't the guts to say so'. Until a matter has been thought out, it's best to say nothing: when it has been thought out, to say frankly or, at the least, clearly and simply what one thinks or has decided.

in connection (or **connexion**) **with.** About or—if *about* or *of* cannot be used in the particular context—concerning; speaking of. 'In connection with alloys, there would appear to have arisen a deficiency of bronze'=Speaking of alloys, I fear that bronze is short; or simply: Bronze is short. Often a direct approach will eliminate the phrase.

in consideration of this (or **that**). In return; in exchange. Occasionally the right word is *therefore.*

increment. *Increase,* especially of income or capital or reserves. whether material or monetary; an addition—strictly one that results from growth or development. *Unearned increment,* earned by someone's hard work or intelligence in the past instead of by wangling in the present, has for more than a generation been the Aunt Sally of income-tax assessors.

incumbent upon (me), **it is**—especially **I feel that it is . . .** *I must* do something. This cumbrous and pompous locution is, of course, no more reprehensible when used by officials than when used by their subjects.

Indianize. To put Indians into governmental positions held by Britons, as in 'The Secretariat at New Delhi has been almost completely Indianized'. The noun denoting either the process or the practice or the fact is *Indianization*. (Variants: *-ise*, *-isation*.)

indicated, is. Seems necessary. In Britain, still slightly colloquial; in the United States, 'impeccable' jargon.

indisposition. Illness. When *indisposition* denotes a minor illness, it can perhaps be excused; when it serves for any illness whatsoever, it is not only long-winded but misleading. (Dr B. Ifor Evans, *The Use of English* 1949.)

individual, noun. A person—any person whatsoever. Only when a person is contrasted with his family, with society, or with mankind in the mass, are we justified in using *individual* for *person*. (*Modern English Usage* contains an excellent paragraph or two on the word.)

Officials have a further cogent reason for avoiding *individual=person;* the word has two pejorative connotations—it is rather contemptuous and it survives from an age of somewhat oppressive jocosity.

inductee. A person inducted—i.e., initiated—into military service; a person enlisted—especially a recently enlisted person. Compare the complementary **selectee.**

in esse; in posse. *Existent*, or *actual;* and *potential*. Adverbially: *actually*, or *in the fact* or *in reality;* and *potentially* or *as a possibility*. These phrases taken from medieval scholastic philosophy are, in this the twentieth century, both anachronistic and—outside of philosophy—almost incredibly remote.

in extenso. At full length—i.e. *in full*. Compare **verbatim ac lit(t)eratim.**

inform. In the Civil Service—at least until Sir Ernest Gowers salutarily began to harry his juniors—one never told anybody anything: one *informed* him. So much more dignified, don't you know.

infraction. See **infringement.**

infra-structure; hence the adjective *infra-structural.* In the *Britannica Book of the Year* 1951, D. C. Browning, the author of the excellent *Everyman's English Dictionary,* defines *infra-structure* (without hyphen) thus: 'the material backing enabling a higher military command to function and forces to be deployed'; Norman Riley, reporting Mr Shinwell's explanation 'to a baffled House of Commons', omits the word 'backing'. The American magazine *Time,* on October 1, 1951, has the passage: '. . . The NATO Council meeting at Ottawa . . . got a U.S. promise of half a billion dollars for NATO's "infrastructure", i.e. defence installations built in one country, but shared by all': and glosses it thus, 'Formally added to the vocabulary of officialese. Said one minister, "Now, when we disagree sharply with another delegate, we can say 'I'll give you a swift kick in your infrastructure!" '

Strictly, *infra-structural* should connote either 'internal' or 'interior'.

infringement; infraction. When, for a *breach* of social etiquette or diplomatic protocol, or a *violation* of national, or of international, law, an official uses *infringement,* he is not committing jargon but merely being dignified or literary: when he used *infraction,* as in 'Such an infraction of Service regulations will entail dismissal' or 'This raid constitutes an infraction of the treaty between our two countries', he is committing both jargon and pedantry; and that, Sir, is an indictable offence.

inhospitalization. See **hospitalize.**

in isolation. Alone; by itself, by themselves. 'In isolation, such an infringement of the rules of the departmental canteen might have been excused if the officer in question had not, when taxed with it, been so rude.'

initial stages. Beginning; start: **in the initial stages.** At first.

initiate. To begin, to start (something); to set (it) going. For a remarkable instance, see **organizational preliminaries.**

Of itself, *initiate* is a good word. The trouble is that Whitehall and Washington will persist in using it pompously.

in loco parentis. In the place of a parent. 'The trustee is requested to remember that, the child's guardians having gone away, he is expected to act *in loco parentis*'—an unnecessary Latinism more properly applied to the guardians than to the trustee.

in my (or **our, his,** etc.) **opinion it is not** (e.g., **advisable**). I do not think it (e.g., advisable). George Orwell mentions an aggravated form of the *opinion* nuisance: 'It is easier—even quicker, once you have the habit—to say *In my opinion it is a not unjustifiable assumption that* than to say *I think*.'

in one's function as or **of.** See **function.**

in perpetuum forms the Latin original of the English *in perpetuity* and should be discarded for it.

In perpetuo arose from a confusion of *in perpetuum*, 'for ever' but also 'forever' (constantly), with *perpetuo*, 'constantly', 'forever' but also 'for ever, for always'.

in posse. See **in esse.**

in pursuance of; pursuant to. In carrying out, in the prosecution of (e.g. one's duties); after, according to, conformably. These legal-sounding, but in fact rather literary phrases are obsolescent, even in the British Civil Service. Yet Washington employs *pursuant to* as a variation of **subsequent to,** as those trenchant ironists, Masterson and Phillips, tell us.

inquire; enquire. Just as an official *informs*, not *tells*, so he *inquires* (or *enquires*), not *asks*.

in rare cases. Rarely. So why write three words for one and why try to break the back of that perdurable camel (quel chameau!) nicknamed *Case* with yet another offensive straw?

in reference to. See **reference.**

in regard to. See **regard.**

in relation to. See **relation.**

in respect of. See **respecting.**

in short supply. See **short . . .**

inspired. An *inspired statement*—perhaps I should have written *pronouncement*—is a statement authorized by a national government and vitiated by shameless or, at best, subtly misleading propaganda and tendentiousness.

inst. or **instant.** See **ult.**

instance. 'Whenever in your reading you come across one of these words, *case*, *instance*, *character*, *nature*, *condition*, *persuasion*, *degree*—whenever in writing your pen betrays you to one or another of them—pull yourself up and take thought. . . .'

'*Instance.* In most instances the players were below their form.

'But what were they playing at? Instances?': 'Q', *On the Art of Writing*, 1916.

This fault occurs very often in officialese.

institute the necessary inquiries. To make inquiries; to cause questions to be asked. This pompous verbosity belongs also to a rather high-flying sort of commercialese. (Owed to *What a Word!*)

institutional; institutionalized. 'On the one side we have the free personality. . . . Its desires . . . are transparent, for they are just what institutional approval keeps in the fore-front of consciousness': cited, by George Orwell, from an American periodical. (A psychological usage.) Compare

'Having, or characterized by, institutions either charitable or educational': adaptation of part of Webster's definition of *institutional.*

Institutionalize clearly means 'to impart the character or nature or appearance of a charitable or educational institution to', e.g., a society. But what a horrible word! Yet even more horrible is the derivative jargon, *institutionalization.*

instrumentality of, by or **through the.** By; by means of; through; because of. 'By its instrumentality, humanity has been preserved'=By this means humanity has been saved. 'By the instrumentality of jargon, the cause of civilization has been retarded by a hundred years'=Jargon has set civilization back by a century.

insuperable objection; insuperable obstacle (or **difficulty**). An unanswerable objection; an impossibility.

integrate, integration. In his essay on 'Words in Vogue' (*Words at War: Words at Peace*, 1948), Eric Partridge quotes from the June 29, 1942 issue of the *Daily Telegraph,* wherein 'Peterborough' had this paragraph: 'After a noteworthy career of some seven years the word "co-ordination" is fast becoming de-moded in the best political quarters. Any M.P. who wants to keep abreast of the times is now careful to speak of "integration". So much is the word to the fore in Ministerial statements and Whitehall announcements that I suspect a co-ordinated—I mean integrated—move to secure the adoption.' Nowadays we even *integrate the hospitalization services.* These two words have been adopted from psychology ('an integrated personality').

For the various 'official' senses, see **consolidate.**

intention is that, the or **the Department's,** etc. The Department, the Minister, we, etc., intend to . . . or that . . . A characteristic official circumlocution.

interavailability. Sir Alan Herbert, in 1935, quoted from a

Great Western Railway pamphlet the magic words, 'Inter-availability of tickets between the G.W., L.M.S., and L. & N.E. Companies'.

Since then we have had **non-availability** and **over-availability.** Soon, probably, we shall receive *disavailability* and *re-availability;* but perhaps we already have them and I've been so lucky as not to see them.

inter-denominational. Sir Alan Herbert has precisely no time at all for these *inter*-monstrosities. He quotes and, with enviable reticence, comments thus: 'Steps should be taken to form a council, on an inter-denominational basis (gosh!) with the object of . . .'

Read: *a council, from all sects*, or even, though the *non-* is not commendable, *a non-sectarian council.*

interested party (or **parties**), **the.** The person(s) concerned. (Does this neutral phrase derive from the legal *the party of the first part, the party of the second part?*) Not that *the person(s) concerned* is much better! To name the 'parties' would remove the offence.

interim. An interval. Compare **hiatus.**

interim arrangement or **measure** or **solution.** A provisional, or a temporary, arrangement, etc. Usually, however, *makeshift* will do the job.

interstitially. Peter Edson, in an article entitled 'Tops in Gobbledygook Is Just About Reached' (*New York Sun*, January 7, 1950), quotes from a governmental pamphlet, *Business and Government*, this splendid example: 'Under one system of law and administration many adjustments to new situations are made interstitially without organic reconstruction of the legal framework.' He comments: 'The word "interstitially" means "in the cracks", and why they don't use short words like that to say what they mean is hard to guess.'

interventor. What most of us would call either an *intervener*, an *interceder*, or, in an industrial or a legal or a political dispute, a *mediator* or, as is the fashion, an *arbitrator*. The word comes from Church Latin.

in the case of. (Cf. **case.**) Sir Ernest Gowers has (*Plain Words*, p. 21) deplored that decay of simple prepositions which has been caused by the official fondness for 'vague phrases such as *in relation to*, *in regard to*, *in connection with* and *in the case of*'. Sir Arthur Quiller-Couch had already derided this egregious example: 'All those tears which inundated Lord Hugh Cecil's head were dry in the case of Mr Harold Cox': with the comment, 'Poor Mr Cox! left gasping in his aquarium!'

in the event of. 'Legal opinion has been taken in regard to whether, in the event of such amendments being made [=if these amendments were made], there would be any possibility of . . .': quoted by Professor J. Y. T. Greig in *Keep up the Fight for English* (1946). In the United States, the usual form is *in the event that* (Masterson and Phillips).

in the initial stages. See **initial stages.**

in the interests of. Officialese for *for the sake of* or even *for*. Compare the quotation at **hypothesis.**

in the majority of instances. Usually; mostly. Included by Sir Ernest Gowers in a short section entitled 'Circumlocutory Expressions of Number'.

in the matter of. 'In the matter of unemployment because of injury or illness, the Commissioners have initiated a policy of clemency' =The Commissioners have said that unavoidable unemployment should be treated sympathetically.

in the near future. See **future . . .**

in the present circumstances. At present; now. Even *in the circumstances* is preferable, *present* being superfluous.

invariably. Always. For some odd reason, officialdom has a marked weakness for *invariably*. Compare 'It is the *invariable* practice of this Department to stagger the holidays of the personnel' = This department staggers the staff's holidays.

investigation; e.g., **make investigation.** To his juniors in the Civil Service, Sir Ernest Gowers has said, 'You may find yourself writing that the Minister . . . will *cause investigation to be made with a view to ascertaining*, when what you mean is that he will *find out*'.

involve the necessity of (doing something). 'Such a step involves the necessity of the Minister himself being present' = Such a step requires the Minister to be here (or there); or, *necessitates* the Minister's presence.

ipso facto. By this (or, that) very fact; by the fact itself; or, by the act itself. In some contexts, the sense is: by the very nature of things. The English phrases are preferable: they are English and they are more precise.

-ise, verbs in. See **-ize.**

issuance. An issue—i.e., *issue* correctly used. Contrast:

issue, noun, as in 'sabotage the Peace issue', adduced by Sir Alan Herbert in his spirited attack on *sabotage*. The word is often used, as here, where there's no need at all for it.

No less often it displaces some far better word, such as *matter, affair, question, dispute, difficulty*, as in 'The issue between them is whether to go to war or to remain neutral'.

it is clear that. 'It is clear that emergency measures will have to be instituted (or, initiated)' = Clearly we must prepare for (e.g., war, the worst, a crisis, etc.).

it will be noted that. See **noted.**

-ize or, in a few verbs, **-ise** (see *Modern English Usage* at -ISE).

Sir Alan Herbert, in *What a Word!* (1935), battled furiously against the indiscriminate coining of verbs in *-ize*. See pp. 52-58 of that entertainingly castigatory work: '*Ize-mania*'.

A few examples occur in this glossary: e.g., **cannibalize,**

cubicalize, deinsecticize, de-ratize, desterilize . . ., all included less on account of the particular horror (the formation in *-ize*) than on that of the general ugliness or unsuitability or unnecessariness of the words as a whole.

J

juncture; especially, **at this juncture,** at this (or that) point; at present; now (or, then). Sir Alan Herbert has quoted 'The Italian standpoint is that at the present juncture the League has no *locus standi* in the dispute': The Italians think that, at present, the League has . . . (This, by the way, was back in 1935).

L

lachrymatory (American, **lacrimatory**) **gas.** Tear gas. To object to *tear* on the ground that, to the eye, it might set up an ambiguity would be stupid: anyone who knew anything about gas would also know which noun was meant.

lay the foundations of is jargon for 'to *found*'. Compare the quotation at **radical transformation.**

leave out of account. To omit; to disregard; to ignore; to forget. Compare **take into account.**

length of time, the. The time; how long. 'It is difficult to estimate the length of time it will take.'

level, at a high (or **higher**)**; at the highest level** (or **levels**). By an official high, or higher, in the Civil Service, or by any high(er) authority; by the Minister, or between two or three Ministers, or, if the matter be still more important, by the Cabinet. 'This is a matter to be decided only at the highest level'; 'Such decisions will be made at the highest levels'; Masterson and Phillips give, as an American example, 'At the childhood level humans like candy'.

[**liable to** do something; **liable to,** exposed or open to. 'He is liable to speak too long'=He is likely, or he tends, to speak too long. 'It is liable to damage'=It is exposed to damage; or, It is easily damaged. A widespread misuse, not peculiar to officialese.]

liberalize. To free (an industry, an activity) from official controls. The principle or the practice or the fact has, all too naturally, come to be called *liberalization*. Both verb and noun have, in 1950-52, been, except among theorists, superseded by **de-control.**

liberee. (American.) A person freed from prisoner-of-war detention. Compare **returnee.**

liquidate, liquidation. 'The far-fetched word *terminate*, having superseded the familiar *end*, is itself being superseded by the more far-fetched *liquidate*. The word is now apparently regarded as suitable for denoting the ending of anything from massacring a nation to giving an employee notice. It is perhaps the worst current example of a word of vague import superseding precise words. . . . Politicians and the Press are at present greater offenders than officials,' Sir Ernest Gowers, *Plain Words* (1948). In general, *liquidation* means no more than 'destruction'. Compare the informative paragraph in *Usage and Abusage* (p. 356) and Sir Alan Herbert's terse reference to it as a 'septic verb'. The first adequate definition of its modern nuances apparently occurs in the Addenda of the 1944 edition of *The Shorter Oxford Dictionary*.

liquid refreshment. A drink. This elegant variation of *a drink* or *drinks* is being laid, not on the carpet of the rotund bureaucrat, but on the desk of the pompously genteel, not entirely literate, Local Government officer, as when, for instance, a mayoral banquet or reception is being discussed.

literally. The authors of *Modern English Usage*, *What a Word!* and *Usage and Abusage* have all spoken uncomplimentarily of this word—not, of course, of its correct use. But *literally* is so rarely used correctly. To equate it to *positively* or *decidedly* or *very* or *extremely* or any other vague intensive is to show oneself ignorant of what it means. This fault is by no means peculiar to officialdom. Officialdom, however, does abuse the word far too often.

literatim or **litteratim.** See **verbatim.**

live, adjective. 'To ascertain the existing live demand for houses'=To find out how many people still want houses (Sir Ernest Gowers, *ABC*). Perhaps from the live wire of electricity.

load-shedding. Such a reduction in the supply of electricity as will prevent too much strain being put upon a generating plant.

In itself, *load-shedding* has merit; what people object to and what, in effect, makes it jargon, are the evasion and the euphemism of the term.

locality. A place. 'In such a locality, it will be advisable to sterilize a large area.' (See **sterilize.**) Compare:

location is an Americanism for **locality,** which is jargon for *place;* nevertheless, it occurs sometimes in English. In 1935 Sir Alan Herbert quoted a report issued by the Ministry of Health and containing the belief that the offer of certain advantages 'would probably secure that industry would adopt the location desired'. (Note the misuse of *secure* for *ensure.*)

locus standi. A right to be heard, especially before Parliament or in a law court. As a legal technicality, the term has legal, if not linguistic rights; used in any other way, it is an abomination.

lucrative employment, in; gainfully employed; both with the verb 'to *be*'. In the language of the jargoneers—in this instance, men earning salaries in the Treasury and especially in the Inland Revenue—these phrasal terms are synonymous. All they mean is, to *earn a living;* to *receive wages* or *a salary.*

M

maintenance of facilities. Maintenance or, better, upkeep.

major, adjective. Overworked by Civil Servants, to the detriment of 'big' or 'large', 'chief 'or 'main', 'important' or 'significant'. (Gowers, *ABC.*)

majority of instances, the. See **in the majority . . .**

make an approach to. To approach. 'It was felt that an approach should be made to X' =It was felt that they should approach X=They decided to approach X.

make application to (someone). To apply to. 'Prospective personnel will make application to the Secretary.'

make contact with. This is one of George Orwell's 'operators' or 'verbal false limbs'. Compare **render inoperative.** In Standard English: 'to *meet*' or 'to *arrange to meet*' or 'to *succeed in meeting*', as the context demands.

maladjustment; mentally maladjusted. Lack of intelligence—lack of sense—inability to live an ordinary life—unwillingness to co-operate with others; insane or, at the best, mentally unbalanced.

For a 'prize' example of *mentally maladjusted,* see the quotation at **organizational preliminaries.** Both the noun and the phrase exemplify the quadruple tendency of officialese to be pompous, erudite, imprecise, euphemistic.

malnutrition. A euphemism, beloved of economists, for *starvation* or, at best, *virtual starvation.* As 'A. P. H.' once caustically remarked, 'We do not hunger or starve; we exhibit evidences of malnutrition, or our diet is characterized by protein deficiency'.

mandatory. (Most American.) Obligatory; necessary.

marginal land. Such land as costs much money to bring it to fertility and to keep it sufficiently productive to further the national agriculture. (Based upon the *Britannica Book of the Year* 1951.) For this sense of *marginal*, compare the *margin*, or *marginal field*, or psychologists.

materialize. To *take place* or *come about;* to *happen* or *occur*. This absurd and unnecessary word, far from being confined to the Civil Service but equally far from being eschewed by Civil Servants, has occasioned a torrent of undiluted scorn. Among its contemners are 'Q', H. W. Fowler, Professor J. Y. T. Greig (*Keep up the Fight for English*), Eric Partridge and Sir Ernest Gowers.

matter of, in the. See **in the matter of.**

matter of prime (or **paramount**) **importance that, it is a.** 'It is a matter of prime'—or, if the matter be urgent, 'the utmost'—'importance that a preliminary report should reach the properly constituted authorities with a minimum of delay'=A preliminary report should go promptly to the authorities.

maximum, adjective. 'As for our modern politicians, whenever they are in a mess they rush for succour to the "dead" languages. The situation is saved by a *moratorium*, a *referendum* or a *quota*. . . . They declare a *maximum* tariff or a *minimum* wage,' Sir Alan Herbert, *What a Word!* (1935). In his *Usage and Abusage*, Eric Partridge is rather rude about *maximum*.

Compare **minimum.**

measure, noun. 'This good word is much overworked in politics and gets a strange new job every day,' said A. P. H. in 1935. It has for some years been much overworked in the Ministries and Departments. Usually another noun can take its place—to the immense benefit of sense and precision.

medical practitioner. A *doctor* or, when one needs to discriminate, either a *physician* or a *surgeon*. (Dr B. Ifor Evans has, in *The Use of English: A Primer of Direct English* [1949], remarked upon this sort of practitioner.)

memorandum; plural, **memoranda.** As an *informal summary* or *statement* or *report* or *communication*, or as a *formal note* (instead of a formal letter), the word can be defended, for although it is pure Latin, well! so are many other English terms. It becomes jargon only when it is used either trivially or outside its generally accepted orbits.

mentally maladjusted. See **maladjustment.**

minimize. To belittle; to underestimate. Strictly, 'to reduce to the smallest size or amount or degree; to estimate at the lowest permissible amount or sum or value', *minimize* should not be, as by too many officials (and laymen) it is, degraded to='to *decrease*, or *diminish* or *lessen*', as, for example, in 'The Minister does not seek to minimize the danger'.

minimum, adjective. The smallest possible or permissible; the least. 'The minimum savings compatible with the nation's financial wealth is *x* millions *per annum*'=The nation must save, yearly, *x* millions—or perish.

minimum calory intake. A modest appetite; especially, only so much food as might satisfy that meagre appetite which the theorists, the airy planners, deem proper to a well-regulated robot. Also see the quotation at **demonstratee.**

mission. The American Air Force's application of the term to a special task or duty, especially at the front (*combat area*), is jargon—but not jargon to which anyone other than a purist would object. The word becomes objectionable only when one of the Services extends it to cover a mere *tour of duty*.

moratorium is a necessary word in the senses 'an obligatory delay; a permissive delay': that is, whether in Law or in Banking. But it has been known to break bounds and to be employed by officials in quite trivial contexts.

motivate, motivation. 'He was motivated by social prejudice'; 'Political motivation frequently masquerades as moral indignation' or 'The motivation of his secession was obscure': read 'He was moved by—i.e., he acted from—social prejudice'—'Political motives are often disguised as moral indignation'—'The reason for . . .' or better, 'Why he seceded, we do not know'. The terms belong to educational psychology and to psychiatry.

multilateral, drawn up—or shared—by more than two states or nations, has something to be said for it, as in 'a *multilateral treaty* or *pact* or *agreement*'. But officials must guard against extending its use.

Compare **bilateral** and **unilateral.**

[**multiplace** is included because of its latent powers for evil. At present it is, I hope, confined to an aircraft that has room for a crew of more than two. It's an obscene hybrid: to a cultured ear and eye, it is a monstrosity.]

multiplicity of, a. Many. 'Owing to a multiplicity of causes' =for many reasons.

mutualize, mutualization; or **-ise, -isation.** To render co-operative,in the sense in which a Co-operative Society is co-operative. It is also employed occasionally as the verb corresponding to the socialistic theory of *mutualism,* defined by *Webster's* as 'advocating a social organization based on common ownership, effort, and control, and regulated by sentiments of mutual help and brotherhood'; the last eight words are merely theoretical.

N

nationalized. State-owned; State (adjective). To *nationalize* an industry is to turn it into a State-owned concern, of theoretical interest to all collectively and of practical interest to none personally. The noun is *nationalization.*

Cf. **denationalize.**

nature. (Cf. **character, condition, description.**) 'Q' cites this passage: 'There can be no doubt that the accident was caused through the dangerous nature of the spot, the hidden character of the by-road, and the utter absence of any warning or danger signal': upon which he comments, 'Mark the foggy wording of it all! And yet the man hit something and broke his neck!' The man met his death because the place itself was dangerous and the by-road was not shown.

necessarily is often employed unnecessarily. In 'A change of government does not necessarily mean a change of rulers' *necessarily* is necessary; but wherever the omission does not basically change the sense, *necessarily* is usually otiose, as in 'He may not necessarily know what has happened'. The word is long and strong: and too many officials yield to its meretricious charms.

negative; especially, **in the negative.** 'Has a Minister to say "No" in the House of Commons? Some men are constitutionally incapable of saying no: but the Minister conveys it thus: "The answer to the question is in the negative". That means "no". Can you discover it to mean anything less, or anything more except that the speaker is a pompous person? —which was no part of the information demanded,' Sir Arthur Quiller-Couch in a lecture delivered at Cambridge on May 1, 1913, and reprinted in *On the Art of Writing* (1916).

Similarly, *yes* becomes *the answer is in the affirmative*.

[**network.** 'Any system of related but not necessarily inter-connected units; e.g., a network of naval bases' (J. M. Wyllie in *The Britannica Book of the Year* 1950). But here we have a term as admirable as Mr Wyllie's definition of it: apt, short and thoroughly English in form. Included altruistically, *pour encourager les autres*.]

nomenclature becomes jargon when it is made to signify something other than 'system of naming', as in 'the Linnaean nomenclature', or 'the terminology used in a science or in technics': and too many officials do lead the word astray in a regimented dalliance.

non-. Officialese tends to overwork *non-*. (But then it tends also to overwork *de-* and *dis-* and *re-*.) 'A. P. H.' has rightly assailed it (1935) with wit and vigour, and Norman Riley condemns it (1951) thus: 'A food firm is asked for "non-undeodorised edible fat", a pharmacist for "non-brushless shaving cream". Is it possible that cooking fat and ordinary shaving cream were meant?'

non-aggression. After scarifying *de-*, *dis-*, *non-* (see the preceding entry), Sir Alan Herbert says, 'I confess . . . that I do not know how "a pact of non-aggression" could be otherwise described'. Why not simply 'a peace treaty' or 'a pact of friendship' or even 'a pact of mutual aid'?

non-availability. (Cf. **interavailability** and **over-availability.**) Lack; as in 'The non-availability of adequate supplies of raw materials'=the lack of raw materials.

non-compensable. Sir Ernest Gowers quotes the following

sentence from an American official paper: 'The non-compensable evaluation heretofore assigned to you for your service-connected disability is confirmed and continued': upon which he drily remarks, 'This means... that the veteran to whom it is addressed has been judged to be still not entitled to a disability pension'.

non-disincentive is one of the worst of the *non-* compounds against which Sir Alan Herbert inveighed in the middle 1930's. As Norman Riley has cuttingly asked, 'Has anybody time enough on his hands to work out what "non-disincentive" means . . .?' Although it obviously forms the negative of **disincentive,** which is an enfeebled negative of *incentive* or encouragement, yet *non-disincentive* does not form an exact synonym of *incentive,* for it merely connotes, or at least should connote, something 'not discouraging'.

non sequitur, sentence; **non-sequitur,** noun. It does not logically follow; something illogical, an instance of bad logic. An outdated remnant of medieval scholastic Logic.

norm. The jargon of Communists and 'fellow travellers' for the normal—in fact, the least permissible—output of work by a worker in a communist country; hence, a normal output in a non-communist country.

normal; normally. In *The Use of English* (1949) Dr B. Ifor Evans has shown how easy it is for officials to slip into unnecessary or incorrect *normal* and *normally.* He selects these two sentences:

'The alternative of attendance at a hospital . . . should be the normal rule,' where *normal* is superfluous;

'Thus, they normally incur considerable indirect expenditure'—upon which he comments, 'The writer here means *always.* If he means *always* the context itself will supply the meaning. . . .'

normalize is, Sir Alan Herbert thinks, permissible as a

technicality of the steel trade; he also thinks that, used in any other way, it is a horror. I have noticed a tendency among officials to use it in non-technical contexts.

normally. See **normal.**

noted that, it will (or **should**) **be.** This is a circumlocution of the kind that possesses an irresistible attraction for Whitehall. Usually they have no merit apart from that of padding: and padding has no merit. (Sir Ernest Gowers quotes several illuminating examples: *op. cit.*, p. 43.)

not in a position to. See **position.**

not prepared to. See **prepared.**

not too distant. Near; close—**in the not too distant future.** Soon.

nuclear reactor. See **reactor.**

number of cases, in a. Often. Compare **in the majority of instances.**

nuptials. A wedding. Often applied by Whitehall—and the Press—to the marriage service of royalty, the nobility, and film stars. Compare **obsequies.**

O

objective, noun. An aim; a purpose.

obsequies is an elegancy, popular among officials and among the genteel, for *burial service.* (Compare the euphemistic *interment* for *burial* or *funeral.*)

observed by a perusal of, it will be. Sir Ernest Gowers has deplored this lengthy variation of *you will see by reading.* Compare **peruse.**

occupational hazard. A risk necessarily run in one's work. If incurred, the risk may bring injury; it may bring disease —*occupational disease.* The latter term can hardly be avoided, but I'm less sure about the former and I'd prefer either *occupational risk* or, despite its lack of euphony, *work risk.*

of even date. Of today. (Adopted from commercialese.)

opinion, be of the (e.g. **same**)**; be of the opinion that . . .** To think—to think the same thing or the same as someone else—to think that . . . The fact that this particular verbosity belongs also to commercialese does not excuse those numerous officials who fall into it as into a feather bed.

opinion, in my. See **in my opinion . . .**

optimum, adjective. For a particularly repellent example, see **beddage.** An excellent anonymous attack upon official jargon was made by the *Evening Standard* of August 17, 1951 in an article entitled 'Optimum Wordage'; Norman Riley has included it in a list of verbal unfortunates; but the initiator of the attack was Sir Alan Herbert in that load of dynamite which he consented to call *What a Word!* Despite all that its defenders can find to say, this piece of barbarism means 'best'.

order, noun. 'Q' scourged *order* in the example he adduces: 'The mesalliance was of a pronounced order': where *of a pronounced order=pronounced,* i.e. (*very*) *bad.* This use of *order* should be compared with **character, condition, degree, nature,** which 'Q' himself brought forward and castigated in *The Art of Writing.*

organizational preliminaries. Preparations. Concerning the officialese of Government departments, a reviewer in *The Listener* of April 10, 1947 remarked, 'They "initiate organizational preliminaries" instead of making preparations. They "integrate the hospitalisation services by the rehabilitation of mentally maladjusted persons".'

otherwise, for *other.* 'What we must ensure in the Welfare State, otherwise than the welfare of almost half the nation, is the virtual certainty that only the members of the Government, and those who implement their orders, shall be reputed intelligent.' This misuse is not confined to officials, but they do perpetrate it much oftener than one would expect of such well-educated and intelligent persons.

output priority. See the quotation at **adequate standard of living.**

outstanding. Excellent; valuable; eminent. A darling of American bureaucracy.

overage is an entirely unnecessary synonym for the good English word *glut.* Admittedly it is better—almost anything would be better—than **over-availability.** Probably formed on the analogy of **coverage** (scope, extent, distribution, etc.).

over-all, usually **overall,** adjective. Predominant sense: 'general'. An anonymous reviewer in *The Listener*, April 10,

1947, mentions that *overall* 'now appears in every paragraph of every Government report' and 'is very dear to political journalists'. He notes that 'the word . . . is applied recklessly to figures and even situations. Inclusive figures are now always called "overall figures", which they are not. . . . "The overall figures of the lower-income brackets" is typical economists' English today'. He ends by saying that 'Economese' is a theme well worth the attention of a certain opponent of officialese. A year later, Sir Ernest Gowers spoke perhaps even more severely of the misuses of this adjective and mentioned an amazing tautology—*overall average.*

over-availability. 'There used to be a simple, forthright word "glut". It generally meant that the public would not or could not afford something, that somebody had made a commercial blunder. . . . There is never a glut with "bulk" buying. It is always an over-availability, an overage, or a customer-resistance when the heroic public palate rebels against the Ministry of Food's latest dietary adventure,' Norman Riley in his scathingly witty article, 'Dehydrated English'. On every count, *over-availability* is a shocking word: and its coiner must have been a man with no feeling for language and (16 letters instead of 4) no sense of economy.

P

panel discussion. A meeting. An American journalist has scarified this piece of American jargon: 'Sample: "Looking toward an ultimate co-ordination and implementation of heretofore diversified interdepartmental practices regarding the briefing of smaller consumers relative to their allotment status, it has been determined that there will be conducted Thursday next a panel discussion in which will be . . ." It means: "A meeting will be held Thursday".' (Frank Aston's article in the *New York World Telegram* of April 6, 1946.) Words fail me.

paramount. *Of paramount importance* has been so debased by jargon that it now means little—anything?—more than *important*.

parasite is included, for it affords an excellent example of socialist—and communist—jargon of a sort infiltrating into general official jargon; it has already been heard from supposedly responsible Ministers of the Crown. In the *Daily Mail*, September 10, 1951. Lane Norcott, in his serial article 'Modern English Misusage', ironically defines *parasite* as 'a person who can keep himself and his family without State assistance or the backing of a trade union'—obviously an exceedingly dangerous person: he not only fends but thinks for himself.

partake of. To eat. This phrasal verb is doubly objectionable: always, because it is an elegancy; often it is misused, as in 'Being alone, I consoled myself by partaking of a glass of stout'. *Partake of* means 'to take one's share of, to share in', as in Dickens's 'Your papa invited Mr R. to partake of our lowly fare'. (Eric Partridge, *Usage and Abusage.*)

partially. Partly. As officialese, more usual in the United States than in Britain.

paucity. This term, which I notice being increasingly used by officials, is a learned word, a literary word ('He exhibits a marked paucity of imagination'): too dignified for everyday use, especially when it means only 'insufficiency'—'lack,' 'dearth'—'fewness'.

pelletize. To form pellets; (transitively) to make into pellets—'said mostly of plant seeds enclosed in small soluble capsules . . ., along with various plant foods to facilitate growth' (Funk and Wagnall's *New Standard Year Book for* 1950). Scientific rather than official jargon—but only too likely to be adopted by governmental experts in agriculture.

pending. Until—but only in such a sentence as 'Nothing can be done, pending the Minister's decision'.

per. See **dietary,** last sentence.

per annum—per diem—per hebdomadem—per mensem. Respectively, *per year—per day—per week—per month;* better, *by the year—day—week—month,* or, because they can be used both adverbially and adjectivally, *yearly—daily—weekly—monthly.* These Latinisms are outmoded. Also, they are superfluous.

per capita. Literally, by heads; for each individual, individually; share and share alike. Used adjectivally: individual; having equal shares. Another unnecessary Latinism.

percentage is becoming very common for *proportion,* as in 'A substantial percentage of the world-population subsists under peace conditions': Most people live at peace. The trouble goes further, *a percentage of* meaning no more than *some*: in this respect, as Sir Ernest Gowers has noted, *a proportion of* also means *some*. In the example concocted by A. P. H., the wordiness of 'under peace *conditions*' is not to go uncondemned.

See also the reference at **substantial.**

per contra. On the contrary; on the other hand, on the other side; offset against this (whatever has just been said). A superfluous Latinism. The word finds an 'honoured' place in Sir Alan Herbert's 'Dead Languages' section.

per diem. See **per annum.**

per hebdomadem. See **per annum.**

[**peripheral** lies on the frontier between the technological and the scientific, on the one side, and—a transferred use—the literary and the official, on the other side. It means 'pertaining to the periphery—the external boundary or the outer surface or the distance round the area or the object concerned'; hence, 'situated on the boundary'. The term is objectionable only when it is made to signify 'marginal'—as official jargon tends to make it.]

per mensem. See **per annum.**

per pro., occasionally **per proc.,** is short for *per procurationem*, by procuration—i.e. by an agent, by proxy. A principal signs; underneath and preceded by *per pro(c).*, or *p.p.*, comes the agent's signature. Sometimes the principal's name is typed, provided the agent's is signed by the agent himself.

per se. Literally 'through'—i.e., by or of—itself; hence, in itself, intrinsically; hence, essentially. '*Per se*, the principle is admirable, but in practice it can easily lead to injustice.' A phrase that seems to fascinate both philosophers and government officials.

personnel. Staff; employees. In Britain it began in the Services.

perultimate, 'concerning or denoting a size, a value, a condition, that cannot be exceeded or improved', as in 'a perultimate crop of wheat from a certain farm'. (The *per-* is intensive.) Admittedly it is much shorter than *potentially the best* or *finest* or *greatest* or *richest;* yet it does rather smell of the lamp and of official pomposity.

peruse. Both an elegancy and a piece of official jargon for 'to read'. Strictly, *peruse* is inaccurate in this sense: it should mean 'to read carefully from beginning to end'. The noun *perusal*—cf. the entry at **observed**—can usually be rewritten in the form 'a *reading*'.

phantom order. A provisional but official order, or set of instructions, to be executed only in a specific national emergency (especially, war).

picture. Situation; rather, idea of a situation. In Britain: Services' slang. In the United States: jargon. Masterson and Phillips quote the sentence, 'The committee gets the picture from this memo'.

pinpoint. From the application to bombing has come the American jargon 'to *pinpoint* the training of students', i.e. to give them a highly specialized training. (The *Britannica Book for the Year* 1946: events of 1945.)

plottage. The area of a plot of land. (The deplorable result of an illicit union between *plot* and *acreage*.) Compare the equally horrible **beddage** held up for derision by two London newspapers within the space of five weeks during the summer of 1951.

point of view. On p. 40 of his astringent and able book aptly titled *Plain Words*, Sir Ernest Gowers refers to the official fondness for *point of view, standpoint, angle*, as 'devices for avoiding the trouble of precise thought'. He quotes: '*From a cleaning point of view* there are advantages in tables being of a uniform height' (italics mine): and proposes *for cleaning*. Perhaps the sentence could be recast thus: 'For cleaning, tables might well be of one height.'

portion. A part.

position to, not in a. 'Various methods are in vogue'—among officials—'of softening the curtness of *will not* or *cannot.* The commonest are *is not prepared to, is not in a position to, does not see his way to,* and *cannot consider.* Such phrases as these are no doubt dictated by politeness, and therefore deserve respect. But they must be used with discretion,' Sir Ernest Gowers, *Plain Words* (p. 40).

Then there is the fluffy use of *position,* as in 'A position will soon be reached when we shall have to act, whether we wish to or not'=Soon we shall be forced to act.

posterior to. After. A 'gobbledygook' variation of **subsequent to.**

practically. This word, apart from its literal sense, means also *virtually,* which, in literary contexts, is preferable; or *almost* or *nearly,* which, in non-literary contexts, are preferable to *practically.* In *What a Word!* Sir Alan Herbert attacked it with gusto and almost with violence—a very practical violence.

The adjective *practical* is often confused with *practicable.* This, however, is a fault not specifically nor even predominantly official.

predecease, to die before, was a euphemism understandable in Victorian and Edwardian days. After the wars of 1914-1918 and 1939-1945 it seems impossibly legal and mealy-mouthed. (Sir Ernest Gowers includes it in a list—p. 22—of *don'ts.*)

prejudice, noun and verb; **prejudicial.** Where *harm* or *to harm, hurt* or *to hurt, damage* or *to damage, injury* or *to injure* can be used for (*to*) *prejudice,* public officials would do well to use them and cease running *prejudice* to death. And in what is *prejudicial* superior to *harmful?*

prepared to admit or **say, not to be.** A polite form of 'I will not say' and a euphemistic form of 'I reject, refuse, your request, etc.' Compare the quotation at **position.**

Also comparable is *be prepared to admit,* or *say,* for *to admit* and *to say.* A. P. H. is scathing on the subject.

pre-requisite seldom means more than **requisite**: and *requisite* itself is usually an unnecessary synonym of *need* (or perhaps *necessity*).

presence on the scene. 'His mere presence on the scene would help to reassure the crowd of frightened people'=His presence would . . . Although this particular example of tautology is not (any more than tautology in general) confined to official jargon, yet it does serve to indicate one of the worst characteristics of much jargon.

[**pressurize.** To supply air to (a sealed cabin in an aircraft flying at over 12,000 feet) by means of a pressurizer or supercharger; to aerate at high levels. So far, *pressurize,* though ugly, is nothing worse than a scientific technicality. Unfortunately, it's the sort of word that bureaucrats adopt and then distort to new senses, often remote from the original.]

prima facie. At first sight or view; at, or in, (its) first appearance; ostensibly. Hence, an adjective, as in 'He has a *prima-facie* case'. To legal and official eyes, the phrase may look well. To anyone else's, it seems—rather, it is—indefensible.

prime importance. See **matter of . . .**

priority. A preference; a preferential rating, especially in that order of importance which the government determines for the delivery of goods needed in national defence or, after 1945, for the general interests of the national welfare. By 1946 the sense had degenerated to '(a matter of) urgency', as in 'The man-power of industry has become No. 1 priority'. All loyal to the cause of good English would do well to heed the verdict expressed in Eric Partridge's *Usage and Abusage*: 'Like *ceiling* it is to be treated with great disrespect.'

prior to. Before. This phrasal preposition belongs, in almost equal parts, to journalese, commercialese, and officialese. But at least it is so common among officials that Sir Ernest Gowers has felt it necessary to warn his juniors against it.

probably eventual. Probable. 'The probably eventual liability of a community'=the probable liability of a group.

probative. (American.) Probable. With thanks to Masterson and Phillips.

problem. Used as an adjective instead of 'difficult' or 'restless' or 'distressed'—as in 'a problem area'.

proceed. To go. ' "Proceed" was a fine word once—a dignified word to be kept for dignified occasions. "Then shall the Bishop proceed to the Communion." . . . But now the whole world "proceeds"—and even "proceeds to go"; and those who merely "go" or "pass" have become the dignified exceptions' (Sir Alan Herbert, 1935). In our fighting Services, a man never goes, whether on leave or transfer or tour of duty, from one place to another; he *proceeds*.

procure, to get by care and effort, to gain or win, has, by the official debasers of a fine language, been weakened, so that now it usually signifies merely 'to get'. As Dr B. Ifor Evans has remarked, 'The simple word *get* may not be very beautiful but it can often take the place of longer words, such as *procure* and *obtain*, without any ambiguity' (*The Use of English*).

productivity. A new word (1930's in the United States; early 1940's in Britain) meaning exactly what is meant by *productiveness;* usually *output* will do just as well—and better. Beloved of economists and Stakhanovites.

pro forma, for (the sake of) form, as a matter of form; merely formally. This mainly commercial Latin phrase (as in 'a *pro forma* invoice') has invaded the jargon of the Treasury: and, wherever it may be used, it could easily be discarded.

proportion of, a. A part of; better still: some. See also **percentage** and the reference at **substantial.**

proportions, especially, *of such proportions,* so big, so large, and, rather less reprehensible, *of such proportions as to . . .,* of a size such as to—usually, however, in the sense 'so big, or large, as to'.

It should be compared with **character, degree, description, condition, nature,** which likewise occur in vague and wordy phrases substituted for exact and single adjectives.

proposition. '*Proposition* in the sense of *plan* or *project* has hardly emerged from the slang stage,' Sir Ernest Gowers, *Plain Words* (1948). (In America, it has long been accepted; in Britain, it is still colloquial.) Its use in jargon has been exemplified by Sir Ernest thus: 'Decentralization on a regional basis is now a general practical proposition': he glosses this extraordinary sentence with the words, 'is now generally feasible'. But *decentralization on a regional basis* could have been shortened to *regional decentralization.*

pro rata. Proportionately; according to the share (whether in credit or in debt) of each member of a group: when *proportionately* will not serve, *fairly* will. Yet another Latin phrase that we could do better without.

protagonist should be used—that is, if it be used at all—to mean the chief actor, the principal, in a drama (the literal sense) or in a conflict, preferably a great conflict. It does not form the mere opposite to *antagonist.* Yet officialdom, and politicians representing officialdom, have adopted it from over-ambitious, would-be 'literary' journalists. In Masterson and Phillips, *Federal Prose,* it is ironically recommended as a substitute for 'an *advocate*'.

protein deficiency. See, at **malnutrition,** an arresting quotation from Sir Alan Herbert. For another example of government dieticians' jargon, compare:

protein ratio. 'Once a politician or "social worker" has acquired the phrase "protein ratio" or "vitamin content" he will never, in public, speak of ordinary food again,' Sir Alan Herbert. As in the preceding entry *deficiency* could have been spelt *lack*, so here *ratio* could have been written *share* or *part*.

protocol. As a technicality in diplomacy and in law, the term is unexceptionable, but its adoption, by the ordinary Civil Service, is deplorable. What is wrong with *formula*, *preliminaries*, *precaution(s)* and the other words that *protocol* is tending to displace?

provenance. This literary word for the usual *source* or *origin* has been insinuating its sleek way into official jargon.

provided that. If; if only. 'Provided that the material is available, the building should be erected without further delay' = If the material is available, the building should go up—*or* be put up—at once.

prox. See **ult.**

psychic; psychological. Emotional; mental—two adjectives that, in Federal prose, are outmoded, official fashion now preferring '*psychological* or, better, *psychic*' (Masterson and Phillips).

public enemy. (American.) A criminal.

purchase, verb. To buy. As a dignified word, it is unobjectionable: but why must officials so persistently use it when *buy* would serve? Sir Ernest Gowers, I notice, warns them against it.

purport, noun and verb. Meaning (or implication); gist. To mean; to profess. 'However obscure the details may be, the general purport, at least, is clear.'—'The writer of this letter purports to interpret public opinion.'

pursuant to. See **in pursuance of.**

Q

quantify and its derivative noun, **quantification.** To measure, in the senses 'determine, ascertain, the quantity of; to estimate the size, the weight, the number of'; to state in terms of quantity; to rate or appraise. It is clear that any of the synonyms *measure, weigh, count, rate,* etc.—or rather, the particular synonym applicable—is, except for scientists and technicians, preferable to *quantify.*

quota. A part or share; dues; assessment; occasionally, even a proportion; allowance—quantity or number permitted.

R

radical transformation. 'This invasion of one's mind by ready-made phrases (*lay the foundations, achieve a radical transformation*) can only be prevented if one is constantly on guard against them, and every such phrase anæsthetizes a portion of one's brain': George Orwell, 'Politics and the English Language', reprinted in *Shooting an Elephant* (1950).

This virtual cliché seems to appeal to the Civil Service: that is a pity, for *transformation* by itself is, one would have thought, 'radical' enough.

rare cases. See **in rare cases.**

ratiocination. Reasoning; a process of reasoning; logical thought; a logical argument. According to the fourth leader in *The Times* of October 12, 1951, 'an American Fowler' has attacked 'such words—or "near-words"—as "build-in inflation", "disincentive" and "ratiocination" '.

rationalize; rationalization. To render scientific; to direct or manage (e.g., a factory) scientifically—where, by the way, *scientific(ally)* is pretentious for *methodical(ly)* or *sensible* (*sensibly*). This thaumaturgic process is ambitiously and very grandly known as *rationalization.* In *What a Word!* (pp. 71, 72, 147) Sir Alan Herbert inveighs delightfully against this pair of pompous noodles.

re- has a useful and honoured place in normal speech. Jargoneers, however, splash it about with a ludicrous profusion and an alarming lack of discrimination: compare, in the ensuing pages, **recategorization, re-decontaminate** (see **re-de-**), **re-deployment, renegotiation, re-validate.** The abuse of *re-* affords A. P. H. some of his wittiest invective.

reaction is included in Sir Ernest Gowers's list of long and overdone words. He glosses it simply as 'opinion, view'. Sir Alan Herbert has attacked it, but rather in its political aspect (cf. the next entry). It has, however, been noted by Eric Partridge that, in addition to the senses 'opinion' and 'view', there exist these others: 'attitude' and 'sentiment'; 'answer' or 'response': and, in the form *reaction on*, 'influence on (or upon)'. The Civil Service appears to contain many persons countenancing and even perpetuating these slack misusages of *reaction*. 'The Minister wishes to ascertain the reactions of the electorate.'

reaction, forces of. Tories or, if you prefer, Conservatives. Socialist jargon of a type unfortunately penetrating into the fastnesses of the Civil Service. Compare the quotation at **entertainment value.**

reactor (1947) or **nuclear reactor** (1946). Any atomic pile in which the scientists can determine and control the amount of atomic energy that is to be, or is being, produced. A *breeder reactor* (1948) is an atomic pile producing more energy than is needed to keep the pile working. (*Britannica Book of the Year* 1950.) American scientific jargon, slowly becoming general among bureaucrats.

re-adjustment looks fairly harmless and in most ways it is: but when it serves as a euphemism for a forcible alteration of mankind's mode of life, it becomes jargon of a rather horrible kind.

rebound; better written *re-bound.* To re-mark the bounds, especially the boundaries (of a region, a province, a country). It is too late in the day to object to Latin *re* tacked to

Germanic *bound;* but, unless the context were simple, one could hardly deduce the sense.

recategorization. 'A "class" becomes a *category*, especially in such an order as "The officers of this unit will appear before the Medical Officer on Tuesday, with a view to a revision of their medical category", though the latter part of the sentence may be jargonized to "with a view to recategorization",' Eric Partridge, 'In Mess and Field. The Jargon and Slang of Army Officers'—in *Words at War: Words at Peace* (1948).

receipt of, be in. To have received (a letter); to be receiving, to receive (pay). Officialese has borrowed from commercialese this flabby piece of verbosity. The use of such terms by officials has been very strongly deprecated by Sir Ernest Gowers.

recivilianized, be. Of American ex-servicemen: to be returned to civilian life and restored to civilian status.

reconditioned. *To recondition* is jargon for: to renovate—repair—restore—make good again, as in 'a *reconditioned* aircraft'; to re-educate (persons); to change (a person's) habits or emotional attitudes. The second affords an example of educational, the third of psychological jargon; both, however, are fast becoming familiar to the bureaucrats.

reconstituted, adjective. Restored to its original nature. At the end of his brilliant attack upon the worst excesses of British gobbledygook, Norman Riley has suggested that witty and amusing opponents might do more to check it 'than has so far been done by more earnest opponents of this reconstituted dehydrated English'; compare Webster's definition of *reconstitute:* 'to restore the constitution of, as dehydrated vegetables or fruits by treatment with water'.

recreational facilities. Games; playgrounds, sports grounds, games rooms; grounds (etc.) and equipment. See the quotation at **entertainment value.**

recrudescence. Revival or renewal; return or repetition. Adopted from the loftier sort of journalese.

rectification of frontiers. 'Millions of peasants are robbed of their farms and sent trudging along the roads with no more than they can carry: this is called *transfer of property* or *rectification of frontiers*,' George Orwell, 'Politics and the English Language' (here, he is attacking the mealy-mouthed euphemism of much official jargon)—in *Shooting an Elephant* (1950).

re-de, as in **re-decontaminate** and its fearsome offspring, **re-decontamination.** This is overdoing things! Two prefixes, as in *decontaminate*, are enough; to add *re-* is to produce ugliness and laughter; and why not say 'to *clean again*' or 'to *clear of gas again*' or whatever else is intended?

Compare the entries **re-** and **re-adjustment.**

re-deployment. Such re-organization and subsequent improvement of a group of factories as will ensure—or, at the least, tend to ensure—greater efficiency, hence a greater output.

redundant. Superfluous, excessive, unnecessary. In the Services, *redundant* came, a little before the War of 1939-1945, to mean 'in excess of the number appointed by establishment' or, briefly, 'in excess of establishment'; during the war, it was—as it still is—applied equally to men and material. 'These uniforms are redundant.' *Webster*, 1934, has the term, used in Engineering Design, *redundant member*, which it defines thus: 'In a framed structure, a member or part not actually necessary for stable equilibrium.' Compare:

redundantize. To declare (something) to be superfluous; to despatch or transfer or sell it as being superfluous. Although this atrocious verb sprang naturally from **redundant** so early as 1944 (late) or 1945 (early), it did not infect Civil Service English until 1948 or (early) 1949.

refer back. This childish piece of tautology, hardly surprising in those who have no Greek and less Latin, does not, one gladly admits, occur among educated Civil Servants.

reference to, in or **with.** Official (and commercial) verbosities for *about* (or the inferior *concerning*) or *for* or *in*, as the context demands. The long-winded *to which reference has been made*=*already mentioned.* Compare the entries at **regard** and **relation** and **respecting.**

reflectorize. To impart, or to supply, a light-reflecting surface to (some object or material). This barbarism was recorded in *Britannica Book of the Year* 1949 as having been coined in 1947.

regard, as in **in** (or **with**) **regard to—as regards—regarding.** About; on; in; for. 'With regard to—*or*, as regards—politics, we feel that they are irrelevant'=Politics are irrelevant. 'Regarding textual criticism of the proposed treaty, he can hardly be accepted as an authority'=On textual criticism, etc. Both 'Q' and Sir Ernest Gowers attack these verbosities and adduce some painful examples. Some people think that unnecessary pain should be avoided.

rehabilitate, rehabilitation. To cure; to heal; to restore (to health); to repair. A cure, a healing, restoration (to health or effectiveness). For a good example, see **organisational preliminaries.** Sir Ernest Gowers has paired it with *recondition* as an instance of a long word ousting a short, good one understood by all.

reinstate, to restore, to re-appoint; **reinstatement,** restoration. In *The Daily Telegraph* of October 8, 1951 appears this paragraph, the last in Peterborough's column for that day:

'The following notice has recently been put up by the

L.C.C. in Lincoln's Inn Fields on land enclosed to let new grass grow:

This ground is temporarily closed for grass to become established after reinstatement.

Evidently some seeds of the Whitehall jargon plant have reached County Hall.'

relating to. Compare **concerning** and **regarding** and:

relation to, in. 'Do not say . . . *concerning* or *in relation to* when what you mean is *about*': Sir Ernest Gowers to fellow Civil Servants. Compare the entries at **reference—regard—respecting**—and:

relative to. *Relative to* is merely a variant of *in relation to*: for a horrible American example, see the quotation at **panel discussion.** Compare **respecting.**

relatively. 'The most indecent adjectives are, it seems, those of quantity or measure, such as *short* and *long*, *many* and *few*, *heavy* and *light*. The adverbial dressing-gowns most favoured are *unduly*, *relatively* and *comparatively*' (Sir Ernest Gowers)—adverbs usable only when a standard of comparison has been mentioned or, at the least, implied.

remilitarize. 'To prepare or equip again with military forces, defences, etc.' (Webster): yet *militarize* usually means 'to render (a people, a country) excessively military in its attitude', not 'to prepare them, or it, for war'. To *equip again*, or to *prepare again, for war* seems preferable to this jargon of the 1940's and after.

remunerate, remuneration. To *pay;* as noun, *pay*—often preferable to *wages* or *salary;* often more precise: *fee*, both noun and verb—or, if you don't like 'to *fee* (someone)', to *pay* (him) *a fee*. The noun *remuneration* occurs far more often than the verb *remunerate;* it seems to officials and others to be so very elegant.

render. To make. To *render a return*, which is ludicrously tautological, means to *make a return* (or *report*, etc.). In the sense 'cause to be', *render* is acceptable—and brief.

render inoperative. To disable (a person or a machine); to supersede (a plan or a process). '*Operators* or *false verbal limbs.* These save the trouble of picking out appropriate verbs and nouns, and at the same time pad each sentence with extra syllables which give it an appearance of symmetry. Characteristic phrases are: *render inoperative, militate against, make contact with, be subjected to, give rise to, give grounds for, have the effect of* . . .': George Orwell, in *Shooting an Elephant* (1950).

rendition. In *What a Word!* Sir Alan Herbert has a short but pungent section on this horror. *Rendition of returns* (or *reports*) seems to be the combination most popular with officials. See **render** above.

renegotiation has, in Federal Prose, a specific sense, defined by the 1945 *Britannica Book of the Year* as 'the renegotiation by the government of original contracts to bring them more in line with actual costs as revealed by experience' (I. Willis Russell, who assigns its birth to the year 1943).

repercussion, usually in plural. A *result*—an *effect*—a *consequence*—especially if indirect, multiple and, like the egregious boomerang, bouncing distressfully back upon the utterer or issuer. See especially *Plain Words* (p. 57) for a delightful essayette.

require. To *need*, to *seek*, to *ask for;* to *ask* or to *order*, as in 'The Minister requires you to attend a special conference, to be held at 1500 hours'.

require detailed consideration. To need to be carefully weighed or scrupulously examined.

required information, the. The information (often, *facts*) you seek or have asked for. 'This Department has endeavoured to obtain the information you require (or, required), but without success' = This Department has tried in vain to get the facts you need.

requisite. (Cf. **pre-requisite.**) 'We do not say "What is wanted is . . ." but "The requisites desiderated consist in . . ." (And requisite, I see, in The *Times Literary Supplement*, has grown to "prerequisite", though in the particular sentence the "pre" adds nothing)': A. P. Herbert, *What a Word!*, 1935. Properly, a *pre-requisite* has to be obtained or fulfilled before a *requisite* can be attended to. In short, *pre-requisite* is rarely permissible.

reside; be in residence. To *reside* = to dwell or, familiarly, live. To *be in residence*, therefore, is worse—much worse—than *reside*, which is pompous or, in certain contexts, dignified.

A *residence* can usually be displaced by *home* or, in formal contents, *dwelling*.

respecting; in respect of. About; on, in, for. 'Do not say . . . *regarding*, *respecting*, *concerning* or *in relation to* when what you mean is *about*': sage and timely advice from Sir Ernest Gowers to juniors conspicuously less sage. Or as Sir Arthur Quiller-Couch, thirty-five years earlier, had said, 'Train your suspicions to bristle up whenever you come upon "as regards", "with regard to", "in respect of", "in connection with", "according as to whether", and the like. They are all dodges of Jargon, circumlocutions for avoiding this or that simple statement.' Compare also **reference.**

respectively. 'He is a member of the Trades Union Council and of the inner councils of Socialism respectively': omit *respectively*, which, like *relatively*, often occurs with a wordy lack of point. Sometimes, as here, *both* could take its place. As Sir Ernest Gowers has shown (*Plain Words*, p. 38), *respective* is correspondingly misused.

responsible for, be. To care for, take care of, attend to, have charge of, oversee. (Catachrestic for) to cause, to have caused.

restore. To give back to a food, e.g. to an *extended* food (see **extend**), the nutritive value it originally had before it was extended or otherwise rendered less nutritious. The 1944 *Britannica Book of the Year* says that the term was first used in 1939. An Americanism.

reticulate; hence, **reticulation.** To distribute, e.g. goods, over an area by means of a transportation 'system'. By the way, one can speak of reticulating either the goods or, by transference, the area. Mr Partridge tells me that he was once—on the strength of a single example—charged with being 'addicted to the reticulated sentence'.

returnee. (American.) A serviceman returned from abroad. Compare **liberee** and **separatee.**

re-validate (or one word). From a document put out by the Ministry of Supply, Sir Ernest Gowers has quoted 'It should be borne in mind that sub-contractors may need re-authorization . . . for sub-authorizations for earlier periods, so as to revalidate orders or parts of orders', where *re-validate* could be written *renew*. Strictly, *re-validate*—if it be used at all (but must it?)—means 'to make valid again'. Often it=*re-issue*.

revolvement has rightly been chosen by Norman Riley for special ridicule. Perhaps he saw it in the *Britannica Book of the Year* 1950, where, without comment, it is defined as 'a changing round, especially the systematic renewal of ageing stocks'. The term belongs to that particular branch of jargon which has been named *economese*.

rodent operator. A professional rat-catcher. The guilt attached to this term (and, indeed, proved by it) lies at the door, not, I believe, of the Civil Service but of Local Government. Mr Riley aptly compares the pomposity of *flueologist*. For euphemism, however, both of these terms must bow to 'char*lady*'—not, I hasten to add, coined by the Civil Service nor used by it.

roll-back. A price-reduction to below the retail level, made in order 'to relieve a "squeeze" on the operating margins of manufacturers, wholesalers and retailers'. This term, apparently recorded first in the Funk and Wagnall's *New Standard Encyclopedia Year Book for* 1942, was coined by the Office of Price Administration. In nature and form, it belongs to the same order of words as **down-turn** and:

run-down. A regulated reduction—for instance, in the number of men in any or all of the fighting services.

S

sabotage, verb. To *spoil* or *harm;* to *ruin;* to *wreck:* any of these words is preferable to *sabotage;* and, correctly used, each of them is more precise. Sir Alan Herbert thinks it a foul word; so do all other self-respecting persons.

same, noun; **the same.** The former, as in 'We require more of same', i.e., 'of the same', is not specifically jargon: rather is it both commercial and almost illiterate. The latter belongs both to commercialese and to jargon; Sir Ernest Gowers, like Sir Alan Herbert and the late H. W. Fowler before him, shows its double affiliation. Usually it can be discarded for ordinary, good English *it* or *these* or *those* or *these things* or *those things.*

In brief, it has many features in common with those displayed by **such.**

sanction, noun. In the sense 'coercive measure', a sense proper to International Law, it could be defended, but, even there, it is misleading, for—compare **screen**—it contradicts the generally understood sense. When officials use it outside the realm of International Law, it becomes indefensible.

satisfied that, be; especially *not to be satisfied with.* To think or believe; especially, not to think, not to believe. 'This Court is not satisfied with the evidence given by the last witness'; 'The Department is satisfied that everything possible has been done to improve the lot of its staff.'

scheduled for discontinuance. 'Certain schools have been scheduled for discontinuance'=Certain schools are due to be closed=Certain schools are to close.

screen, verb; **screening,** noun. Harold Ward, in the Glossary at the end of the Funk and Wagnall's *New Standard Encyclopedia Year Book for* 1943 (published in 1944) defines *screening* thus: 'In the psychiatric treatment of large groups of individuals, . . . the process of weeding out all those whose condition is such as positively indicates physical or mental breakdown, or failure to adjust themselves to the responsibilities of military or other exacting service. Also as a verb, *to screen*.' Later: to pass candidates (especially those for the Civil Service or for atomic research) through a test designed to determine both the promising and the unfit—or the politically unsuitable. The term comes, not from *screen*, to shut off light from, to protect, but from the mining term *screen*, to sift (e.g., sand or gravel).

secure, adjective. Safe. So too *security* for 'safety'.

secure, verb. To ensure. In another sense: to get. 'It is anticipated that the Minister will secure that there shall be no further difficulty'=The Minister is expected to ensure that there shall be no more trouble=The Minister will (we expect) see that there's no more trouble.

see one's way to; especially, *not to see one's way to*. A Minister's secretary or personal assistsnt avoids exposing his chief to the simplicity of 'The Minister cannot grant your request': instead he says, 'The Minister does not see his way to granting (*or*, acceding to) your request'. Admittedly, he wishes to be polite. But must he also be euphemistic?

selectee. In general, anyone selected; in particular, a person called up for service (e.g., in the American Army) under the selective system. American jargon, originally; soon, I fear, to be also British.

separate; separatee. A *separatee* is one who has been *separated*, i.e. either discharged or released from service in the American armed forces. This is done at a *separation center*.

seriatim. Why officials—though less than before 1939—should prefer this piece of Medieval Latin to the English *serially* or *in series*, one hardly knows, unless it be that the word looks impressive and learned.

serve no useful purpose. See **would serve . . .**

serve the purpose of. This phrasal and long-winded verb occurs in George Orwell's frightening list of 'operators' or 'verbal false limbs', designed to save thought and to give an air of symmetry to a somewhat vague statement.

servo-mechanism is perhaps scientific rather than official jargon for *auxiliary mechanism*, any mechanism either independent of or merely attached to another, but helping to make the latter more, or more diversely, efficient.

set-aside. (American.) Such supplies, especially of meat and vegetables, as are set aside by the government for its own use.

shortfall in supplies. A shortage. For a condemnatory quotation, see **underdelivery.** Compare:

short supply, be in. (Compare **shortfall** and **underdelivery.**) 'My schoolgirl daughter, unforgiven, talks of milk chocolate being in short supply when she really means there is none at the shop,' Norman Riley in *The Daily Telegraph* of July 14, 1951. The economists introduced this wordy synonym for *scarce* or *unobtainable.*

signature, under one's or **the.** Signed by. Perhaps it is quibbling to suggest that a letter is, in the fact, *over* the signature, for *signature* did formerly mean a seal; and also a *sign manual*, or royal signature, does come at the top of the charter or royal grant.

sine die. Without a date appointed (for, e.g. Parliament) to meet again; hence, 'adjourned *sine die*'=adjourned *indefinitely*. True; *indefinitely* is longer than the Latin *sine die* (literally, without a day), but it is at least English.

sine qua non. An essential, a necessity—which is precisely what one cannot claim *sine qua non* to be.

situation resembles **position** and **condition,** in that, employed in order to avoid bluntness or abruptness, they all result, or tend to result, in obscuring the meaning. For instance, 'The situation will eventually be restored' is less precise and less re-assuring than 'In the end, all will come right'. (Adaptation of a paragraph in *Plain Words.*)

situation difficult to surmount: a difficulty. **Situation impossible to surmount:** an impossibility.

spallation. 'The act or process of reducing to fragments' (Funk and Wagnall's *New Standard Encyclopedia Year Book for* 1947). Technological rather than Civil Service jargon. What's wrong with *fragmentation?* Presumably this barbarous word derives from the mining and masonry technicality, to *spall*, itself from *spall*, a fragment or chip (Middle English *spalle*).

special area. An objective, outsiders' definition is this, from the New Words section of *Webster*: '**special areas.** Certain sections of England and Wales forming the subject of special legislation because of disproportionately severe depression and destitution'. A Whitehall term, common in the 1920's and 1930's; extant, but rather less used since 1945.

specific. Particular. Usually it is superfluous, as in 'This specific rule lays it down that . . .' (See especially Sir Ernest Gowers, *ABC.*)

spiral; price spiral; inflationary spiral. So long as these terms are kept by economists within the strict bounds of economics, they remain technicalities—difficult, perhaps, yet irreproachable. But I have, during 1950-52, noted a tendency for them to be loosed from those bounds: to become, in short, official jargon.

spot authorization. A War Production Board (U.S.A.) procedure, by which local agencies are authorized to grant to manufacturers the right to manufacture civilian goods if they prove that at least some of their operatives and part of their machinery exceed what they require to contribute to the war effort. 'Coined' in 1944, says the 1945 *Britannica Book of the Year*.

standpoint. See **from the . . .**

state. To say. 'You are hereby directed to state your intentions' ='Please say what you intend to do'. The reason for this use of *state*—cf. **acquaint, communicate** and **inform**—would seem to be a desire to uphold the dignity of the Civil Service and of Local Governments. (Admittedly, many of the latter need some such prop and stay.) Sir Ernest Gowers will have none of it.

status. State or condition. Compare:

status quo, the state existing, things being so (or, as they are), is short for *status in quo*, Latin for '(the) state in which'. Compare the derivative *status quo ante bellum*, the state of things, the state existing, before the war. For example, 'To restore the *status quo* (*ante bellum*) will be difficult.'

sterilize. 'The satellite town, with its wide belt of sterilized land' was quoted in 1935 by Sir Alan Herbert, who pointed out that, here, *sterilized* does not, as you have the right to expect, mean 'rendered sterile, i.e. barren': 'The Town-Planners and Green-Belters, when they propose to "sterilize" a given area, mean that it shall *not* be sterile, that it shall produce *nothing* but vegetation and natural life, as opposed to buildings. It is like saying that you will cultivate land when what you mean is build on it. Very odd.'—'You may already find examples of *sterilized* used merely as a synonym for *wasted*,' Sir Ernest Gowers, 1948. For a similar contradictoriness, compare **sanction.**

stipend, in its restricted sense 'the salary of either a magistrate or a clergyman', is (need I say?) impeccable. To use it of schoolteachers is jargon; to use it of wage-earning minor Local Government employees implies a pomposity bordering upon insanity.

stockist. A *stocker*—one who stocks supplies of goods, e.g. copies of books. *Stockist* is a hybrid, ugly to look at and hard to say. Sir Alan Herbert fiercely (and rightly) attacked the word so long ago as 1935. For *stockists of pianos*, he proposes *we stock pianos*.

stockpile, noun and verb. A stock, a reserve; to accumulate, to maintain, to reserve a stock, especially of tinned food or raw materials or atomic bombs. This Americanism has, since 1949, been making an insidious inroad into official English: a pity; for *stockpile* says nothing more than *stock* (n. and v.) or *garner* (v.) or *save* (v.) or *reserve* (n. and v.) can say equally well—indeed, better.

stress, verb. Admittedly it is English for and shorter than 'to *emphasize*'. Sir Ernest Gowers has, however, rightly selected it as a word overworked in official circles—a vogue word to be avoided.

subjected to, be. To have to undergo; or, merely, to undergo, to experience, to encounter. Perhaps not so much true jargon as an example of an excessive dignity.

sub judice. (Of a lawsuit that is still) 'under a judge'—that is, *under judgement*—that is, in straightforward English, *being tried*. All very well for lawyers; all very undesirable for laymen.

subminiaturization. Gobbledygook, originally scientific, for 'the technique of making even smaller devices, such as radio valves, that are already small' (I. Willis Russell in the *Britannica Book of the Year* 1951); a specific instance is called a *subminiature*.

sub-ration. To ration a commodity—especially clothing or food—to the wholesalers or other distributors, but not to the retailers: 'and God help the poor sailor on a night such as this!'

subsequent to. 'After. With reference to time, prefer *subsequent to*: "The undersigned will be pleased to discuss the matter with you subsequent to lunch". *Following* is also recommended: "Following his marriage he gained weight." For variety use *posterior to* or *pursuant to*,' as we are ironically instructed by Masterson and Phillips in their immensely readable pamphlet, *Federal Prose.*

substantial. Big, large, much, considerable. In *What a Word!*, Sir Alan Herbert mentions *a substantial percentage* (or *proportion*) as commercial long-windedness for 'some, much'. But latterly this word *substantial* has been gaining ground in the official world.

See, too, the quotation at **coverage** and compare **appreciable** and **considerable.**

substantially. Much; in the main. 'The hope has been expressed that, substantially at least, the negotiators will be in accord'=We hope that the negotiators will, in the main, agree.

substitution for, be in. To take the place of; (occasionally) to displace. 'The proposed school will not be in substitution for one or more discontinued schools' (Education Act of 1944).

such. Having, in an attack on his special bugbear, *case*, quoted the sentence, 'It is contended that Consols have fallen in consequence; but such is by no means the case', Sir Arthur Quiller-Couch (*On the Art of Writing*, 1916) remarks that '*Such*, by the way, is another spoilt child of Jargon, especially in Committee's Rules—"Co-opted members may be eligible as such; such members to continue to serve for such time as"—and so on'.

H. W. Fowler, in 1926, castigates users of *such*. He does it with verve and at considerable (yet not excessive) length.

Eric Partridge, 1947, has no long general article upon *such;* he breaks up the attack into seventeen brief, vigorous raids.

The subject is far too large to be treated here. I recommend all diligent inquirers to go to both 'Fowler' and 'Partridge'. But a good working rule is: Never use *such* for *this* or *that,* nor for *this thing* or *that thing—thing* here representing any noun or noun-group.

An illuminating comparison is afforded by **same.**

sufficient. Enough. (Included in Sir Ernest Gowers's list of unnecessary 'longs' for adequate 'shorts'. He might have added *a sufficiency* for *enough* used as a noun.)

supererogatory is what Eric Partridge has called a 'literarism', either for *superfluous,* as in 'These definitions are supererogatory', or for *excessive,* as in 'superergatory attentions'. It is a good word in its religious and ecclesiastical applications, as *supererogatory virtues* and *supererogatory fasts* or other *observances.*

superseniority. (American.) That special seniority which, on re-enlistment, applies to veterans of the armed forces.

supply. See **shortfall** . . . and **short supply.**

supra-national or as one word. Applied to any measure or consideration so important for the world as a whole that it overrides the claims inherent in the sovereign independence of the country concerned. In fact, *world-wide* or *universal.* Norman Riley has included *supra-national* (the British spelling) in a truly hair-raising list of 'Whitehall English' words that, although indubitably 'Whitehall', are certainly not English.

surmount. See **situation.**

T

take into account. (Cf. **leave out of account.**) In 'Politics and the English Language', reprinted, from *Horizon*, in that very attractive posthumous collection of essays, *Shooting an Elephant* (1950), George Orwell has transcribed 'Time and chance happeneth to them all' into officialese:

'A considerable element of the unpredictable must invariably be taken into account.'

In short, *take into account*=to *consider* or to *include*, as the context demands.

take into consideration. To consider; to consider also. (Compare the preceding entry.) 'It is incumbent upon us to take into consideration the possibility that an over-availability of vitamin-adequate provisions will probably render the situation even more complicated'='A glut of good [or, nourishing] food will perhaps make things worse' or, less pithily, '. . . complicate the situation.'

take steps to do something. (Compare the two entries preceding this.) Sir Ernest Gowers to his juniors in the Civil Service: 'You may find yourself writing that the Minister *will take steps to*, when all you mean is he *will*.' So watch it, please: don't go taking steps that may turn out to have been a waste of ink and time.

tangential. (American.) Irrelevant; merely incidental.

tantamount to. This is a rather too literary way of saying 'the same as' or 'equal to' or 'equivalent to'. *Webster's* quotation 'A usage nearly tantamount to constitutional right'

(Hallam)='a usage amounting almost to constitutional right'; 'This is tantamount to stating that the man is an imbecile'='This is as good as saying the man's a fool' (or 'One might as well say . . .').

target for 'figure aimed at'—'figure, or amount, desired'—'goal'—has, since about 1942, been grossly overused by politicians, economists, Civil Servants. (Could the famous documentary film, *Target for Tonight*, exhibited throughout Britain and abroad during the years 1941-1942, have started *target* on its too fascinating journey from near-sense to utter nonsense?) At pp. 58-59 of *Plain Words*, published in 1948, Sir Ernest Gowers shoots unerringly at this often very silly word.

technological has, in economese, a specific meaning: resulting from such improvement in technical processes as renders machines more productive and thereby eliminates or, at least, subordinates old industries and reduces or even eliminates work done by hand. (Modified from *Webster*.) For instance, 'technological economies' or (*Webster*) 'technological unemployment'.

tender one's apologies—condolences—congratulations. These verbosities lie on the marches between Elegance of the genteel kind and a slightly old-fashioned Officialese: and are much used by the inhabitants of both regions. Younger officials, like any other self-respecting person, now say *apologize—condole* (perhaps rather *sympathize*)—*congratulate.*

terminate. Transitively: to end or finish; to conclude; to close.—Intransitively: to stop or cease; or (of a subscription) to expire. Whether transitive or intransitive, *terminate* can nearly always be discarded for one of the above synonyms. So, too, for *termination*: use *end, finish, close, conclusion, stop, expiry.*

terminus a quo and **terminus ad quem.** The end from which, i.e. the beginning or the starting-point; and the end towards, or to, which, i.e. the end or the finishing-point, the destination. These Latin phrases, well suited to abstruse philosophical arguments, especially about causation and serial development, are no longer permissible to Civil Servants—or, outside of philosophy, to anyone else.

thereafter, thereat, thereby, therein, thereof, thereto, thereunder, therewith; hereafter, hereby, herein, hereto, heretofore, herewith. These adverbs and several others like them, common in legal terminology, in Biblical language, and perhaps in a very literary and elevated prose, are best avoided on all other occasions, both by 'ordinary blokes' and by Heads of Departments. Sir Ernest Gowers (*Plain Words*, p. 22) is very sound on this point. Say: *after that; at that point* (or *place*)*; by that means*, or *thus; of it; to it; under that* (*point*)*; with that*, or *after this; by this means, in this; to this; hitherto* or *until now; with this.*

[**throughout the community.** Everywhere; by everyone. This particular long-wordedness is as common outside the Civil Service as within it: but those within should know better than to use it.]

through the instrumentality of. See **instrumentality.**

through the correct—or **usual—channels.** Officially—i.e., according to official procedure; regularly (*not* irregularly).

[**top secret** is the American counterpart of the British *most secret.* Introduced late in 1943 or early in 1944, the term fell into the common domain not later than 1947. Although originally official, *top secret* can hardly be stigmatized as officialese.]

to the effect that usually=*that*, as in 'Our opinion is to the effect that . . .', which='Our opinion is that . . .'=We think that; 'The decision, the document, the letter, etc., is to the effect that . . .'='The decision is that' (=I have decided that . . .) or 'The document, or the letter, says, or means, that'.

to which reference has been made. See **reference.**

transfer of population. Summary—often, brutal—expulsion. See **rectification of frontiers.**

transmit. To forward; or merely to send. Included by Sir Ernest Gowers in his list of lazy 'long 'uns'. Properly used, *transmit* emphasizes the passage from sender to receiver—or from one place to another.

transpire. To *happen;* to *occur.* This doubly horrible verb has been adopted, from journalese, by both commercialese and officialese. There is a good excuse for 'commercial gents'; some slight excuse for 'the gentlemen of the Press': for Civil Servants, merely that of human fallibility. *Transpire* can, with offence only to the most pernickety of purists, be used legitimately for 'to come to light' or 'to become known, especially if gradually', for literally it means 'to be exhaled as vapour or perfume, hence as moisture'.

transportation, as in 'You will be requiring *transportation* to Edinburgh', wastes eight letters; the word needed is either *ticket,* which has six, or *pass.* This is an Americanism that British officials could advantageously have left in America: it is also an Americanism that Americans could well have forgone, for it is 'purist' gobbledygook.

type, noun, is being grossly overworked, in official as in other circles, to the detriment of 'class', 'kind' and 'sort'.

type, verb; **untypable.** To *type* anything is, in the scientific and medical worlds, to determine its nature or, more exactly, its particular type; to identify it scientifically or medically. That which can be so determined is *typable;* that which cannot, *untypable.* The verb was first—and, in the main, still is—used in the medical sense 'to determine the type of a sample of blood', itself from the medical or physiological term, 'a blood *type*'.

U

ult., of last month; **prox.**, of next month; **inst.**, of this month: short for *ultimo mense* (L. *mensis*, a month)—*proximo mense*—*instant* (from *mense instante*). This horrible commercialese was, long ago, taken over by the Civil Service; but true Servants have, since the 1930's, been opposing it. *Of last month*—*of this month*—*of next month*, or the month plainly named: either of these methods is preferable to those Latin 'dead hands'.

ultra vires. Illegal, illegally; exceeding one's rights or powers. This sort of thing may be all right in Law, but it exceeds the limit in everyday matters. Officials should, instead of abusing, abolish it.

umbrage; especially, **take umbrage,** to take offence, to become angry or indignant. *Umbrage* ranks as an elegancy—a rather pompous elegancy—and, perhaps for that very reason, it has seduced many a Civil Servant from 'the straight and narrow'.

un-. Under the ironic heading 'Labour-Savers', Sir Alan Herbert (*What a Word!*) has written thus sagely: 'Most of us seem to suppose that if we take a good word and put dis-, de-, re-, in-, un-, or non- in front of it we make an equally good word. This is not always true.' Civil Servants and Local Government officers share the blame with lesser mortals; and Civil Servants, at least, should know better. Compare the following example from the New Words section of *Webster's;* '**unreconstructed** *adj.* Stubbornly tenacious of the political and economic tenets of an outmoded party or period'.

unavoidable concomitant. 'A certain curtailment of the right to political opposition is an unavoidable concomitant of transitional periods' is George Orwell's rendering into jargon of 'The right to speak one's mind disappears during a revolution'. For *concomitant*, one can usually substitute the much more widely understood *accompaniment* (synonym) or even *result* (approximation).

underdelivery. 'The Treasury, which as the fountain-head of Whitehall's authority should show the lesser breeds beyond Whitehall how to write good English, are another source of hideous and complicated jargon. They use "disequilibrium in the balance of payments" to mean the dollar gap. They use "shortfall in supplies" or "underdelivery" to mean shortage,' Anon., 'Optimum Beddage' in the *Evening Standard*, August 17, 1951.

under present conditions. See **condition,** noun, second paragraph.

under-privileged. Lacking privilege(s), whether social or political or, especially, economic—hence, at a disadvantage (e.g. economically). As *Funk and Wagnalls*, in the 'Supplement' of the 1949 edition, has succinctly defined it: 'Specifically, through economic cause, not privileged to enjoy certain rights theoretically possessed by all members of a community or state.' (No nonsense about earning the rights or qualifying for the privileges.)

under separate cover. Separately. 'The relevant forms are being despatched to you under separate cover'=The forms are being sent to you separately=The forms go to you separately. Probably adopted from commercialese.

undersigned, the. I; we. Compare the quotation at **subsequent to.**

understand, e.g. **You will (doubtless) understand that . . .** To hear; to learn, be informed; to realize; You will see, or realize, that . . .—or, You know or will know . . .

Certainly, in such a sentence as that quoted by Sir Alan Herbert—'The sluices, I understand, are operated by a system of cam-gauges'—it does not mean 'understand'. For a scintillating paragraph upon the precautionary or face-saving use of *understand*, see that writer's *What a Word!* (p. 108).

underwater element. (American—especially in the Departments of the U.S. Army and the U.S. Navy.) A submarine.

undue (alarm); unduly. '*Undue* and *unduly* seem to be words that have the property of taking the reason prisoner. . . . It is, I suppose, legitimate to say "Don't be unduly alarmed", though I should not myself find much reassurance in it. But "there is no cause for undue alarm" differs little, if at all, from "there is no cause for alarm for which there is no cause", and that hardly seems worth saying,' Sir Ernest Gowers, *Plain Words* (p. 36). For another pithily expressed stricture on *unduly*, see **relatively.**

unilateral, unilateralism. One-sided; single—one-sidedness; singleness. '*Unilateral* should be confined to the jargon of diplomacy and physiology, to which it belongs,' says Sir Ernest Gowers, who cites 'We will not adopt a policy of unilateral disarmament', a politician's officialese for 'We will not be the only country to disarm'. Thirteen years earlier, Sir Alan Herbert described *unilateral pact* (or *treaty*) as 'raving nonsense': my only criticism is that he might well have put it more strongly.

unique. Exceptional—or, even, unusual; excellent.

unit. In 1949 this word for anything from a field or a machine or a building to a person began to become popular in the official circles both of Britain and of America. *Unit* is now a famous leveller of people and individualities and distinctions. Probably deriving from the Army's description of battalions, etc., as units.

units of currency. (American.) Cash; coin of the realm.

unquestionably. Certainly, surely; without doubt, without question. Often, however, as Dr Ifor Evans has noted in *The Use of English: A Primer of Direct English* (1949), the word is used where, in the fact, its absence would not modify the sense and would, indeed, strengthen the sentence.

unreconstructed. See **un-**, towards the end.

until such time as. Until. 'Until such time as you are ready, nothing can usefully be done.'

untypable. See **type.**

upgrade, verb. To substitute a comparatively cheap or inferior product for a product of better quality—but charging for the substitute at the higher rate; to raise the price of something without improving its quality. (An Americanism.)

upward adjustment. A flatulent euphemism for a rise in price. Selected by Norman Riley for a (dis)honourable place in a catalogue of crimes against the language.

urgent. Officials tend to use this formerly strong and peremptory adjective as a synonym for 'reasonably important—anyway, not to be put into the waste-paper basket; or, should be attended to before the next committee-meeting or accounting or inspection'. Sir Ernest Gowers has—none too soon—had something trenchant to say upon this abuse.

usage. Of a commodity, especially of a raw material: the amount used or used-up. Industrial jargon of the sort beloved by economists.

utilitor (or **-er**). One who serves as 'handyman' to the president or other high executive of a large business; a trouble-shooter (or 'killer' of trouble). An Americanism recorded first in the Funk and Wagnalls *New Standard Year Book for* 1950. From '*utility* man'.

utilization can always give way to the simple *use* (noun), or, occasionally, *using* (verbal noun); and **utilize,** to the verb 'to *use*'.

V

vend. To sell. 'I know how sensitive the man of business is; but his reluctance to use such vulgar words as "sell" and "seller" is surely nearing the neurotic.'

'A warrior'—one who fights alongside A. P. H. in the good cause—'has caught, outside a new post office in Dorset, this: "Stamp-vending Machine",' Sir Alan Herbert, *What a Word!*

verbatim ac (or **et**) **literatim** (or **litteratim**). Word for word (*verbatim*—from Latin *verbum*, a word) and letter for letter (*lit(t)eratim*: from L. *lit(t)era*, a letter of the alphabet); exactly as spoken and exactly as written.

[**vertical envelopment.** Capture and retention of an area by a force of paratroops and air-borne infantry—usually along with penetration by ground troops. Military jargon, included because it is such as to fascinate, be adopted and then modified by the official mind.]

viable agreement. A practical or a sensible contract. See the quotation at **application of social principles.** *Viable* is an erudite word, unexceptionable in an erudite disquisition or in a literary composition; but not a good word to use in a governmental report or in a pamphlet intended for businessmen.

victuals, for *food,* is an elegancy or, if you prefer it, a genteelism—or it goes near to being one. (Though not so near as *viands* does.) Strictly, *victuals* denotes 'articles of food; supplies of provisions': employed thus, it cannot be indicted. Even when equated loosely to *food,* it is, as jargon, falling into disuse.

view. See **with a view to.**

viewpoint of, from the. See especially **from the standpoint . . . of.** '*View, Point of View.* Current only among niggling pedants and querulous tories. Substitute viewpoint': thus, ironically, Masterson and Phillips.

virement. In the *Sunday Times* of August 26, 1951, J. M. Wyllie, staff lexicographer to the Clarendon Press, writes thus: ' "Virement" is a French word which has been gradually coming into use in English during the last forty years or so as a financial technical term for the authorized transference of a surplus under one head to balance a deficit under another in various public accounts. It has become much commoner since the institution of the National Health Service, but it is still normally pronounced as in French.' It shortens the French *virement de fonds*, transfer of funds (from one article of the budget to another); *virement* derives from the intransitive verb *virer*, to turn or sweep around.

vis a vis—written thus, without the hyphens and without the accent of the French *vis-à-vis*. In Federal Prose, this forms an elegant variation of **concerning** and **regarding.** (Masterson and Phillips.)

visualize is a good word, but, outside of rhetoric or impassioned prose or lofty verse, it should not be used where 'to *imagine*' or 'to *picture*' would convey the sense. Sir Ernest Gowers has included it in his valuable list of long or too-literary or vogue words that could profitably be superseded.

vital. (As officialese, more American than British.) Important; essential.

vitamin content. (See the quotation at **protein ratio.**) The amount of nourishment in a given food. Both *vitamin* in medical and official, and *content* in scientific and official jargon, have been much overdone since the 1920's.

viva voce. By word of mouth; oral. A Latinism that could profitably be discarded. Even an incipient graduate could just as well say, 'I have to go back to Oxford, next week, for my *oral*' as say ', . . for my *viva*'. (Whether he would is another matter or, Americanicè, 'something else again'.)

W

whether or not (you do something). Whenever *whether or not* means, as usually it means, nothing more than *whether*, officials could save typing and paper by preferring the single word. Only when the element of doubt—sorry! I should have written, only when the doubt—needs to be emphasized, will a careful speaker or writer use *whether or not*, for which, incidentally, *whether or no* is obsolescent. (Partridge, *Usage and Abusage*, pp. 328, 366.)

[**while,** for *whereas* or *although* or even *and*, can lead to a very troublesome ambiguity. This misuse is not peculiar to officialese: see especially 'Fowler' and 'Partridge' on usage.]

[**Whitehall English** or **Whitehallese.** See Introduction.]

wildlife. Gobbledygook's word for wild beasts or birds or fish—or even for wild plants. (Masterson and Phillips.)

Will you be good enough to (e.g. **advise me**)? Please tell me. On the score of courtesy, this piece of official jargon is unexceptionable: but isn't it perhaps just a trifle wordy?

winterize. To prepare—to render secure—against winter; applied especially to airfields and aircraft. This aeronautical technicality will, I fear, attract the Civil Servants, so pathetically susceptible are they to verbs in *-ize*: the more exotic and, to the stylist, uncouth the verb, the more fascinating it seems to be.

with a view to; e.g., **with a view to ascertaining.** Sir Alan Herbert quotes 'the raising of the moral and aesthetic standards of the cinema with a view to united action to secure . . .'

which = 'the moral and aesthetic improvement of the cinema in order to obtain . . .', which itself could be shortened. *With a view to ascertaining* = *in order to*—or simply *to—find out.*

with reference to. See **reference.**

with the object of (doing something). In order to (do something). 'A committee is to be formed with the object of discussing the difference between *field grey* and *dark grey*.' A characteristically official lengthiness.

working party. Any industrial committee—originally a Government-appointed committee—consisting of both management and workers and aiming to establish such a policy as will promote the greatest efficiency within the relevant industry. An odd distortion of the literal, natural sense.

worth-while; American: **worthwhile.** Excellent or, at the least, superior; valuable. As officialese, rather American than British.

would serve no useful (occasionally **good**) **purpose** is even more cautiously tender of the addressee's feelings than (*it*) *serves no useful purpose.* Admittedly it is polite: the euphemism, therefore, can be partly excused. One need not be so blunt as to say *It is*, or *would be, useless;* one can say *It does*, or *would, not help.*

Y

Your letter (is) to hand. This adoption from commercialese is being sternly discouraged by all those Civil Servants who regard English as an ally, not as a victim. 'Your relationships with your correspondent are not commercial,' as Sir Ernest Gowers tersely remarks.

You will (doubtless) understand that . . . See **understand.**

You would be well advised to . . . I think you should (do, or avoid doing, something); or, You would be wise, or prudent, to . . .

accrual basis, on an. An american accountancy phrase, beloved of the American income-tax authorities.

animal feeding stuffs. Have the bureaucrats never heard of **fodder?** This shocking ineptitude was strongly condemned by the English newspapers of February, 1952.

computation; to compute. (Mostly American.) An estimate; to estimate.

executivization (or **-isation**). 'This happens, it seems, when acting executive officers are confirmed in rank. . . . Clearly the Civil Service talent for coining extraordinary words still thrives. That they hit the ear with a dull thud is no doubt another matter': 'Peterborough'—who shows 'em up for what they are—in *The Daily Telegraph*, May 21, 1952.

itemize. (Mostly American.) To particularize; to give, or state, in detail.

non-depreciable. Land is so described by the U.S. Inland Revenue authorities. Soon we shall be taxed for having the sublime impudence to breathe. Already, those who are so very odd as to wish for quiet must pay dearly for the privilege.

sanitary convenience. Local Government officialese for a urinal, a water-closet, or even an entire lavatory.